WILL
THE REAL
WINNER
PLEASE
STAND

WILL THE REAL WINNER PLEASE STAND

DALLAS GROTEN

BETHANY HOUSE PUBLISHERS
MINNEAPOLIS, MINNESOTA 55438
A Division of Bethany Fellowship, Inc.

Photos by Dave Tieszen and Dick Easterday

Published by Bethany House Publishers
A Division of Bethany Fellowship, Inc.
6820 Auto Club Road, Minneapolis, Minnesota 55438

Printed in the United States of America

Library of Congress Cataloging in Publication Data

Groten, Dallas, 1951-
    Will the real winner please stand

    1. Youth—Prayer-books and devotions—English.
I. Title.
BV4850.G756   1985   242'.63   85-19993
ISBN 0-87123-819-5 (pbk.)

Will the Real Winner Please Stand

*I asked God for strength, that I might achieve,
I was made weak, that I might learn humbly to obey . . .
I asked for health that I might do greater things,
I was given infirmity that I might do better things.
I asked for riches that I might be happy,
I was given poverty that I might be wise.
I asked for power that I might have the praise of men,
I was given weakness that I might feel the need of God.
I asked for all things that I might enjoy life,
I was given life, that I might enjoy all things.
I got nothing I asked for but everything I had hoped
for. Almost despite myself, my unspoken prayers were answered.
I am among all men most richly blessed.*

—*An unknown Confederate soldier*

Dedication

Born with the dawn, so small and so helpless. But you shouted out to the world with a cry of strength. And at that moment I knew a mighty God would reign within your heart. This book was written during a year forever crystallized within my memory—the year of your miraculous entry into our family. For in your smile I could see the sun; in your beauty I could see your mother; and in your life I could see Christ.

Dedicated to my daughter, Bethany Dawn Groten, and to my wife, Caroline.

". . . Thus God's power always goes forward amid extreme weakness."

—Martin Luther

The Author

DALLAS GROTEN holds a B.A. in sociology from Augsburg College in Minneapolis. He has served in several churches as a lay minister. He was head track coach and is presently a student counselor at Wykoff High School in Wykoff, Minnesota. This is his second book.

Acknowledgments

This book tells a true story. *Will the Real Winner Please Stand* is based on my third season as track and field coach for Wykoff High School in Wykoff, Minnesota, recording triumphs and defeats of that season.

However, in writing I discovered I could not accurately duplicate the inner battles, agonies, and joys of the young men and women who lived through these dramatic events. I could only expand on what they told me they had felt at the time, and fill the gaps with imaginative guesses. "Imaginative guessing" is the core of fiction; therefore, I will call this book a work of fiction based on solid truth.

The defeats and accomplishments of the characters are real. At times, such defeats and victories have been altered to protect, not exploit, the good and kind people of Wykoff. But the characters are fictitious; they are symbols. For instance, Sam symbolizes Wykoff itself, while Sean symbolizes the person who does not go out for sports but is nevertheless a champion. Sherri symbolizes the young woman who has courage to face life when life does not turn out as she had hoped, and Marie represents the person who holds her head high despite ridicule. The list goes on with every character. In all fairness, I must also state that the character of "coach" symbolizes what I have learned about strength and weakness over the years. And the chapters that don't specifically have track and field as their stage are symbols of that learning process.

I would like to express my deep gratitude to the true heroes and heroines of this book, the young men and women of Wykoff. They are people of strength and character who have inspired me. Let me say a special "thank-you" to these champions:

Paul Eberle, Dan Eickhoff, Stuart Scott Eickhoff, Dan Evers, Charlene Hellerud, Dan Hellerud, Phil Kaun, Dale Kent, Todd Kramer, Charles McPherson, Keith Northway, Liam O'Byrne, Mark Rath, David Root, Angela Leonard Shafer, Jim Shafer, Kenneth Shipton, Michelle Sikkink, Paul Vesey, Grace Vomhof, Sadie Winslow, Jeanne Wolfgram, and Terry Wolfgram.

I would also like to express my thanks to Thomas Ames, who gave me a chance to coach, and to my editor, Nathan Unseth, who gave me the chance to write. And a very special thank-you to my parents and my wife's parents, John and Viola Groten and Richard and Ida Griebel, who taught me a great deal about the value of hard work.

—Dallas Groten

Contents

Introduction

As a track and field coach I witnessed how important strength and victory are in the eyes of the world. But a study of the Bible shows that God demonstrates strength and victory in a different light. For instance, in God's Kingdom, victory is found through losing, living through dying, and ruling through serving. The King of Kings entered the world as a helpless baby, referred to himself as a Lamb, listened to His followers call Him weak and foolish, and died powerless on a cross. Even the Apostle Paul said, "When I am weak, then l am strong" (2 Cor. 12:10, RSV).

But you, too, as a Christian, can say with Paul, "When I am weak, then I am strong," because all things work together for the good for those who love God and are "called according to his purpose" (Rom. 8:28, RSV). Yet the conflicts we face living by Kingdom principles in the world can cause much confusion. May this book help alleviate that confusion.

I am not advocating defeat or weakness as a way of life. The Christian, as a member of the world community, should always strive to be a winner in all areas of human endeavor, yet never forget the importance of faith, not human striving, in matters of salvation. "You have been saved through faith." That means we must *trust* only Christ to take away our sins, live His life in and through us, and eventually take us to heaven. In *all* of life, though we may have many weaknesses, God *is* our true strength.

Will the Real Winner Please Stand is not about principles;

13

it's about a Person. In fact, the "principles" presented will work only if Christ is the most important person in your life—your Lord and Savior. Therefore, you won't find a systematic "how-to book." It is only meant to point you to the living Christ and encourage you to seek Him.

As you seek Christ, you will make exciting discoveries on how personally God guides your life with His Word. That is why it is important to be a student of the Bible. To help you, we have included an explanation of a Bible passage in each chapter.

Please read this book from beginning to end. If a concept is unclear in one chapter, it will be explained on a deeper level in another. Each chapter flows together to explore the unified message that "your weakness can be God's strength." I hope this volume will help you see that what you hate the most about yourself can be used by God for your good and His glory.

"He is not weak in dealing with you, but is powerful in you. For he was crucified in weakness, but lives by the power of God. For we are weak in him, but in dealing with you we shall live with him by the power of God" (2 Cor. 13:3–4, RSV).

1

Finding Strength in Weakness

Pain ate into his face.

"I know," he said. "I know. My girlfriend doesn't want anything to do with me anymore. And it's tearing me up. But I've got to go on, don't I? And I will. But in these tough times maybe I don't need inspiration from you. What I need is a swift kick in the pants . . ."

The pain was like a cancer spreading all over him. Can heartache kill? Maybe it won't kill the strong, but who's 100 percent strong every second of every hour?

I could see my own face reflected in the eyeglasses of this young man. As I leaned back in the black swivel chair behind my office desk, I could not take my mind off my image. For behind that image were his eyes, eyes filled with hope, hope that somehow I would have an answer that would wrestle away the horror of his life and cast it into the abyss.

But what can I give you, Dave? I thought. Certainly to one so hungry, I could feed *something*. He knew what I stood for and what I represented, I was the youth counselor of his church, a Christian who tried to live in the power of Jesus Christ, but who was now riddled with doubt by the blaring reality of pain, cruelty, and evil in life. He knew that my trembling finger still pointed to a cross. Yet he needed no clichés, no cute slogans.

"Dave," I said, bending forward, glancing at my wristwatch, "do you mind if we take a quick walk over to your house and maybe pick up this conversation later?"

"Sure," Dave said, swallowing and adjusting his glasses. "But why my house?"

"Channel Ten, KTTC in Rochester, is doing a story on my track team in fifteen minutes. Should be interesting . . ."

Dave was an outstanding student, a good basketball and baseball player, a great outdoorsman, a speech contest champion with a writer's gift for communication. Perhaps such gifts in the past could insulate one from the horrid problems of being young. But Dave stood out as a symbol that *no one* is immune from life's trials. And no one, no matter how strong, is without bouts of weakness.

His mother greeted us with a smile at the front door.

"Mom," Dave said with a rising excitement, "he's going to be on TV."

"Oh, how wonderful!" she exclaimed as she clapped her hands together.

All three of us sat down on a large sofa.

Bold images were soon flashing across the screen. We could see a beautiful all-weather track in a pleasant suburban setting. Muscle-bound, city-bred athletes pranced, leaped, and vaulted in near-Olympic splendor.

I was not only a lay minister, but also head coach for a public high school. And in Rochester, Minnesota, the home of the Mayo Clinic, a television station was doing a story on my team.

But my team was *not* on the screen at the moment. No, those images were of the Rochester Mayo track team, shown by way of contrast.

Now the cameras drifted to our track in Wykoff. Wykoff is a small, rural community, and our team's track was not of all-weather asphalt excellence. It was composed of clay and mud, with dandelions sprouting up between the lanes. I watched the cameras pan the faces of my young men and women, sprinting, jumping and throwing, not in suburban splendor, but on an earthen track a good rain could wash away.

But why a television story about my track team? Why a story about a small team not in contention for the state title, with just one coach who possessed only a year's experience in charge of both boys and girls, junior and senior high, on a primitive track? Why such a story when Mayo's track sparkled in the video sun?

True, we had beaten several teams last season, but we had grabbed only a team first place at one track meet. What's so great about losing that they would want to do a TV story about us? Losers *are* losers, right?

The answer was simple. Our team was worthy of attention because of its weakness. Wykoff's track team found strength in its weakness. And in the track world we had many weaknesses:

One coach, not three or four.

A history of struggle and fight, not a history of trophies and state titles.

A clay and mud track, not durable asphalt.

Few athletes. Athletes who did not go to track camp in the summer to improve their skills, but were burned by the sun in farm fields.

Yet somehow our weakness had been the very foundation from which an enduring strength had emerged. As light cannot shine without darkness, so, too, our strength would not glow before any television cameras without our weakness.

Despite the obstacles, fifty youngsters in our town of 450 were out for track. Such a proportion in a larger school would be staggering. The year before, three-quarters of my small boys' team had advanced to regional competition. And there was every indication, as the TV commentator stated, that our team would continue to grow in strength all season. Such prophecy held true. At the end of the season, Wykoff, the smallest track school in the district, would be district runner-up, taking home the school's first track trophy.

Despite our lack of coaching personnel, despite the facilities, despite size, despite underdog status, Wykoff shouted, "We will do our best!" Our weaknesses were transformed into the strong motivational fireworks that boost champions forward. And every step forward, even if it ended in a last place, we looked upon as a triumph. Our weakness was our strength.

I glanced at Dave. The beaten lines on his face were gone as he sat enjoying the television story.

Later he would say to me, "I feel life spinning all around me. And those sharp edges of life are charging at my guts, to slice me all up. You know, other people look at me and think I'm pretty strong. Me? *Strong?* Right now I don't feel so strong."

I took a breath and spoke firmly. "In God's hands our weakness can be His strength."

Then he leaned so close to me that I could feel his breath singe my face. "But how?" he gasped out. *"How?"*

What About You?

How can your weakness be God's strength?

We often lose in life because of our weakness, but our weakness *can* be God's strength. Yes, "all things work together for good to them that love God" (Rom. 8:28). Therefore your weaknesses and defeats can be the very gifts that will push you into true victory. My track team *did* have many weaknesses. Most of the media would have written us off. But one commentator recognized strength in our weakness. We need to recognize the potential for strength in our weakness. God's "strength is made perfect in weakness" (2 Cor. 12:19). Losing does not make you a loser, because your weaknesses can be God's strength.

This book is not only for athletes. In fact, it's *not* about athletes at all. It's about the exciting person of Jesus Christ, and track and field is merely the stage on which this book is built. Jesus Christ is the one who can transform your weakness into strength.

"But he said to me, 'My grace is sufficient for you, for my power is made perfect in weakness.' I will all the more gladly boast of my weaknesses, that the power of Christ may rest upon me" (2 Cor. 12:9, RSV).

1. What is the common view of weakness?
2. Do you ever feel like an "underdog"? Consider the verse above. What should you do when you feel like an "underdog"?
3. How can your weakness be the foundation of your strength?

2

I Want Superstars, Not Wimps!

The image of the scoundrel began with a simple thought and grew until he stood before me in sharp clarity.

His eyes were dead. Dead from constantly penetrating into others with criticism, sarcasm and pessimism emanating death, not life.

His skin, pale and sallow, had seen little sun as he crouched in press boxes, viewing those warriors of daylight known as athletes. Yes, his body had absorbed too much coffee, too much beer, and too much smoke.

The cigarette dangled from the corner of his mouth, the ash a quarter-of-an-inch long, the brim of the press-pinned slouch hat pulled down over one dead eye. His body was wrapped in an overcoat, even though the spring day was very warm. His back was hunched as he squinted his eyes, bending over an ancient black typewriter, his gnarled, old-before-their-time fingers hunting and pecking the keys, crucifying on paper an innocent seventeen-year-old pole vaulter for a trait he called failure.

He sensed my presence in the press box and cocked his head, shooting one dead eye at me.

"Yeah?" he croaked, the ash of his cigarette falling to the lap of his gray trousers as his lips moved. "What ya want, Scumbag?"

I was furious, but I wanted to keep my composure. If I showed him any human weakness at all, he would crucify me, too, right in the *Sunday Edition.*

I clenched my teeth and the words seethed out of me. "Listen Mr. Riley Hunter, I'm the coach of that young man you're writing about, and I'm here to tell you that you have no right to print that negative trash."

Riley Hunter yanked his dead eye off me. He again bent over the ancient typewriter, his wrinkled hands striking the keys.

"Mr. Hunter," I said in exasperation. "Please don't print that. You're going to hurt innocent people."

He did not look at me, but I could detect a hint of pleasure on his face, pleasure because I was near the point of begging. And that's what he wanted to see: me groveling, crawling to him on my hands and knees.

"Listen," he croaked out. "I'm a sports writer. I'm only interested in the very best. I want perfection, not mediocrity. Superstars, not wimps. I'm looking for the red and beautiful roses of athletic excellence. And in order for me to find them, I have to grip a machete in my hand and slash away all the weeds that hide the roses. Your little pole vaulter is one of those pesty weeds that obstructs my quest and makes my job a pain. So I'm going to slash him to bits." Hunter spat out his cigarette butt, sending the flaming missile zipping past my right ear.

I was furious, but I was afraid of showing that anger. Riley Hunter loomed as a powerful force of public opinion. However, I could contain my rage no longer and shouted, "How can you live this way? To you, the only people worthy of praise are the athletes on winning teams who win first place in every event. You constantly look for faults and never virtues in people. You see only weakness, never strength. You laugh and jeer and condemn us who dream and work to win, who run with bleeding feet over jagged obstacles you have hurled before us. And when we cross the line in second place, beaten by someone blessed with an ounce more physical strength, you spit your cigarette butt at us and embrace the *winner*."

I could tell by the look of scorn on Hunter's face that my impassioned speech had not affected him in the least. He calmly lit up another cigarette. But I could not stop speaking.

"What about us, Mr. Hunter, scratching at your window? What about us who don't wake up every morning rejoicing in our possession of what you call 'strength'?"

I looked at Riley Hunter's ash-burned clothes, his hunched body, his dead eyes, his parched skin.

It was hard for me to believe that Riley Hunter never existed.

What About You?

Mr. Hunter is an imaginary figure, but a voice like his croaks inside each of us when we fail at a task the world tells us we must accomplish. That voice calls us "Loser," "Failure," "Stupid," "Ugly," "Strange," or "Weak." And the more attention we pay that voice, the louder it will scream.

"Please me," it croaks, "and you will please your friends, and the people you want to become your friends—that pretty young woman, that handsome young man . . ."

Yes, Riley Hunter screams inside each of us. And that's why he will continue to be a "character" in this book. You see, Riley Hunter is every voice, both inside and outside of us, that never sees good, that criticizes, laughs at, and scorns. Riley Hunter destroys every flower, every sunset, every breath of love, and every birth.

Riley Hunter sounds like a voice from hell, but oftentimes he is the voice of our own human weakness.

"He that telleth lies shall not tarry in my sight" (Ps. 101:7, KJV).

1. Why is Riley Hunter a liar?
2. Does Riley Hunter exist inside you?
3. What can you do to get rid of Riley Hunter?
4. Are you a positive or a negative person?
5. What can you do to not sound like Riley Hunter to other people?

3

It's Not the Loss but the Gain

"Runners to your mark. . . !"

Electricity fired through every muscle of his body. For weeks he had anticipated this moment. *The regional track meet!*

The sun beat down upon him. The crowd was a tapestry of many colors, many towns, and many faces. And the numerous voices of that crowd rose high to become one voice. A voice smashed into silence by the ragged scream of a stocky man with pistol in hand.

"Set. . . !" The man's arm stretched far above him, the pistol aiming at the beating sun.

The eerie silence on a near-summer day was a devastating silence beating inside the runner's ears and storming through his skull. And in that silence Sam knew that fifteen seconds from now it would all be over.

At the gun, he thought, *explode out of the blocks. Beat him!*

The *him* was strained for action, crouching in the lane next to Sam, an athletic giant in his state and nation. Sam stood in awe of this superstar's skill. And it had been his goal all year to beat *him*. But no one had beaten *him*, for *he* was the champion.

I'll beat him today, Sam thought.

The silence pounded hard. Would it never end? Each young man felt like the trigger of that pistol.

My goal, Sam thought. *A year of pain. Beat the champion!*

Silence.

Crrrack!

The young men leaped out of the blocks. Their spikes pierced the all-weather track. Arms pumping. Eyes arrow-straight. The first hurdle rushing toward them . . .

. . . Just days before, Sam's long fingers had stroked the polished wood and shining brass of Wykoff's first track trophy, won by his team last week at the district track meet. The winning tradition blazed within his soul . . .

He fired out his lead leg. His arm shot straight and forward. He leaned with his trunk, flying into the air. Clearing the hurdle, his feet landed one, two, upon the track. But he was behind most of his competitors.

His feet dug into the track. He blasted forward, hearing the rattle and the knock of hurdles. The silence of the crowd vanished into an ocean of shouts and screams. *Second hurdle!* The waves of screaming enveloped him completely. Third hurdle! He pounded the track, then grazed over the fourth hurdle, soon pulverizing the earth with agile movements of grace and power.

Fifth hurdle!

He sped past one athlete, then flung himself by another. Sixth hurdle! Leg. Arm. Lean. *Perfect. Goal! There, in the distance, the line!* One hurdler dropped behind him. Then another! Now it was just Sam and the champion fighting it out.

Sam's eyes glanced at the massive chords in the legs of the champion who sailed over hurdles to the right-front of him. Soon ground was devoured as Sam's feet ate up the track, reducing the distance between the two runners.

Seventh hurdle!

I can do it, Sam thought. *So close. Can't let up now. All out!*

He lunged with a crashing force, his spikes stabbing the track in competitive violence.

Strain. Sprint! Goal! Not dreams! Real as blood.

Even! Sam and the champion were dead even.

The crowd went wild in a storm of screams.

"C'mon, Sam! C'mon!"

"C'mon, Champ! C'mon!"

The last hurdle loomed closer. *Closer.* The hurdle. . . !

. . . Perfect!

Now it was an all-out, 100 percent, do-or-die sprint.

"C'mon, Sam! C'mon!"

Applause! Step. Step. Strain. Lunge! Lean . . . Victory?

Sam felt a strong, bandlike arm wrap around him. "Great race; you were super," the champion said to him.

And firing from the crowd, a bright-eyed face beamed as she spoke to the young man who had an arm around Sam. "Close race, Champ! You won. But I knew you would."

Then that ugly voice which seems to croak so often in the world, that voice made up of fear, hate, and destruction, jeered inside Sam. Would Sam listen?

"You loser!" it hissed, like a stench from a swamp. "Simple arithmetic. You *weren't* first place. You were second. And only a *first place* can be called winner, right? You *failure*! You failed at a goal you worked a whole year for! He was strong. But you were weak!"

The day was over. The champion was still the champion.

After the race, Sam reached over the mesh fence where I stood. Joy wreathed his face. He wrapped his arms around me and hugged me. He was not sad about failing to obtain his goal. Why? Because his eyes were not set on what he had lost, but on what he had gained.

But just what did he gain?

In Minnesota, the champion in every regional event goes on to the state track meet. But so does each second-place finisher.

So Sam was going on to the state track meet. Not only that, he was the first person in the history of his town and school to advance to a state tournament in any sport!

To the people of Wykoff, Sam was a reigning hero. They were excited about his future possibilities.

"It's not over yet," I told him with pride. "You get to face the champion again next week."

He adjusted his glasses, then smiled his slow, broad smile.

What About You?

Have you failed in sports, school, family, job, social life, or spirit? Have you listened to the condemning voices within you?

Have you looked for excuses by blaming your failure on your weakness?

Take a look at what you have lost. But don't look long. Now take your eyes off what you have lost and put them on what you have gained through that loss.

When you have found the disguised blessing in your adversity, you have caught a glimpse of the character of an almighty God who can bring His victory out of your defeat, and His strength out of your weakness.

"But what things were gain to me, those I counted loss for Christ. Yea doubtless, and I count all things but loss for the excellency of the knowledge of Christ Jesus my Lord: for whom I have suffered the loss of all things" (Phil. 3:7–8, KJV).

1. Think of a loss in your life. What did you gain through that loss?
2. Think of the last time a voice jeered inside you, condemning your weaknesses. Did that voice speak truth, or a mere half-truth?
3. What weaknesses of yours can you use to motivate yourself to success and victory?
4. Can you think of a time in your life when a loss was better than a gain?
5. What can you do to see the gains in your losses?

4

Called to Be Faithful, Not Successful

He was a hero in his hometown. The talk all around Wykoff was, "How will Sam do at the state track meet?"

Sam was a fine young man, an honor student, and a gifted singer and musician. His father was not only the superintendent of Wykoff's Lutheran school, but also the mayor of the town as well.

When Sam's track team shined before the TV cameras, they were fifty strong. But much of that team had been eliminated at district, the rest at region, and he alone would represent the entire team at state.

He *was* the Wykoff track team. The entire town rested upon his shoulders. He would carry the strength, courage, and skill of Wykoff to Bloomington Lincoln's beautiful track. And he knew that such a track was in profound contrast to our rugged oval of clay and mud.

Sam, his friend Pete, and I departed from Wykoff among good cheer. We drove to the Twin Cities, Minneapolis and St. Paul, which to us was massive. And through carefully examining road maps, we found our way to the track of Bloomington Lincoln High School.

Excitement was everywhere—the state track meet!

Our small school had never been able to break out of regional competition in any sport. Sam had been hurdling for only one calendar year. And this was just my second season of coaching. Everything was overwhelming.

People were rushing everywhere in their expensive jogging

suits, lugging their leather duffel bags—all seeming to know where they were going. We, by comparison, stumbled around trying to act like experienced veterans, while our awe and anxiety told a completely different story.

"Tomorrow," I reminded Sam, "is the finals in the 110 high hurdles. You have to get through the preliminaries today if you want to make those finals." Then I told him something he didn't know. "Right before your race today, they'll announce your name over the loudspeaker. When you hear your name, you are supposed to step in front of your blocks and bow to the crowd."

A slow and large grin slid across Sam's face. He adjusted his glasses and his spirit flashed. "This really *is* the big time," he laughed in a deep and deliberate voice.

In the hurried flow of activities, we were rushed through the dressing room, and the next thing I knew the preliminaries were beginning and Sam's name blared over the loudspeaker.

Sam hopped in front of his blocks and bowed to the crowd while I brooded on the other side of the peopled stadium in the coaches' bleachers with Pete beside me.

"How do you think he'll do?" Pete asked.

"The competition's fierce," I said with concern. "The champion isn't in Sam's heat. If Sam does his best, I'll be proud of him."

"He's always given his best before," Pete stated encouragingly.

I squinted across the infield on that overcast day. The runners were in their blocks. And they all looked so small. I could barely pick out Sam.

"For two seasons I've been close to Sam in every race he's run," I said with disgust. "I've been able to shout out a word of encouragement when he's sped past me. But now, now he's so far away from me that I can't even see him—"

The gun cracked in the distance. I could see a gray whisp of smoke.

Starting so soon? I thought. *Everything's happening so fast! I don't feel ready. Does Sam feel ready?*

For months I had shared with him strategies, technique, and motivational helps. But he was so far away from me now, alone, miles away from the Wykoff that was so proud of him. Was all he had learned a part of him now?

All of the hurdlers dived out of the blocks. To me, they looked like a string of ants racing in greed toward a sugar crystal. I strained my eyes to find a gold uniform leading the pack. He was usually in front, but where was Sam now?

He was trapped between two large hurdlers, as three more trailblazed ahead.

Hurdles crashed over and bounced back into place. Lungs grunted and gasped. Short spikes stabbed the black pavement. Heartbeats throbbed up into every throat. All eyes were pasted to the finish line. And every dream aimed at winning.

Sam's face was strained, his glasses sliding down his nose, and his dreams flaming before his eyes. His mind chanted: *Win! Win! Win!* His heart beating: *I'm Wykoff! I'm Wykoff! I'm Wykoff!*

And when that last threatening hurdle was conquered, Sam became the perfect sprinter: his shoulders straight, his arms pumping at his side, his eyes branded to the future. He was doing everything I had told him to do.

At last I could see a gold uniform at the finish line. But when Pete and I spotted that uniform, we knew we would not be at this state meet tomorrow. The glory was gone.

A lying voice screamed inside me: "After that television story, after the runner-up trophy, after almost beating the champion at region, after all the attention they give you back home, you bring your hurdler up to *state* and he doesn't even qualify for finals! He'll go home without even a sixth-place medal. What an outrage! You'll be scorned in Wykoff. Your team is too weak. Go home, Big Fish! Go home to your small pond. Losing makes you a *loser.*"

How does one answer such a truth?

By realizing that it's a half-truth and therefore a lie.

The weakness of Sam's inexperience as state competitor was a steppingstone for the strength of a more experienced hurdler to win the heat. Life does not always seem fair; but based upon his years of training, the winner deserved to win more than Sam did. Sam gave his all, but Sam's weakness was a strength that worked together with the weaknesses of other hurdlers for a common good: *the joy of victory for the first-place winner.* If there were no losers, there would be no winners. Light cannot shine brightly without darkness.

After the race, I placed my hand on Sam's shoulder. "Hold your head up," I said. "You've been faithful to all that I've taught you. You did your best. Our watch says it was your best time ever."

Sam smiled that slow, lazy smile. "Don't forget, Coach," he said, "I'll be back next year."

Sam was the first athlete from Wykoff to go to a state tournament. He started a tradition that continues to this day.

What About You?

God calls us to be faithful, not successful. Do your best at each task set before you, and leave the success and human recognition to God. He blesses the Christian with many gifts.

If you find yourself a loser because of one weakness or another, remember, your weakness has made another strong. Because you are a loser, someone else tastes the happiness of being a winner. Rejoice! God is using you to do His work in the world. He is using *you* to bring joy to another brother or sister.

"We are fools for Christ's sake, but you are wise in Christ. We are weak but you are strong. You are held in honor, but we in disrepute" (2 Cor. 4:10, KJV).

1. Do you agree that if you become a winner in any earthly pursuit, it is in part due to the weaknesses of others?
2. If you agree with the first question, how does this make you feel about your weaknesses? Your strengths?
3. Think of the last time you applied for a job, or tried to win a contest of brain or brawn. How did the weaknesses of others highlight your strength?
4. List specific times in your life where your quest for success has cancelled out your faithfulness to God.
5. What can you do to put your eyes on Christ and not worship worldly success?

5

Youth: Wise or Foolish?

It all seemed so easy to him.

His powerful legs would churn down the blacktop, his arms pumping like iron pistons. His feet hopped, skipped, and jumped. He would fly high into the air. Spectators thought he would continue rocketing skyward forever. But then, at last, down, down he dropped until his body was in the shape of a contorted "L." His feet stretched out before him, his toes struck the earth, and soon his whole body exploded into the sand, pushing himself forward, he braced his fall with his hands.

The measurement? Thirty-eight feet, three and one-half inches.

The distance leaped was remarkable. Keith, the triple jumper, was only in ninth grade.

Keith was one of the reasons I expected to have a good team next season. For Keith was not only an excellent triple jumper, he was also a top sprinter and could fair well in both the shot and discus.

. . . Keith climbed up to the hayloft and walked toward the pile of hay bales. He reached into his pocket for a jackknife, but it wasn't there. He had forgotten the knife in his room, and he needed it to cut the twine off the hay bales.

Keith knew his legs were powerful. They could do wonderful things, like leaping across that oblong opening, the one he had just climbed through.

On the other side of the opening, sticking into a board, was a butcher's knife.

But such a long, long opening, he thought. *And such a big drop below.*

Could he make it?

Then he remembered how people cheered for him at track meets. The cheering stormed his brain.

Yet it would be safer to climb back down the ladder, readjust it, and climb to the other side of the opening for the knife.

But I'm in such a hurry. I have a basketball game tonight.

What would he do?

His powerful legs pounded the loft floor. That dark rectangle he must leap over rushed toward him, closer, closer . . .

. . . There's no take-off board. Where should I start the jump? Maybe I should quit . . .

But then a sneering voice within screamed: "You coward! What are you afraid of?"

For a moment he thought this voice was just like the crowd watching him at a track meet.

But I shouldn't. I shouldn't!

"You can do it! C'mon! You can do it!"

I shouldn't.

"YOU CAN DO IT."

This is foolish!

Would he do it? Would he?

His feet missiled off the floor. High. Higher! Again the powerful surgings of the might in his legs overwhelmed him. Far above the opening, soaring across the sky, he was the King of the Air Hill, sitting upon a cloud in athletic splendor.

But it had to begin now. High can only go so long. He started his fall.

His body shot forward and automatically popped into the "L" position. The edge of the opening . . . the hard floor to safely land upon . . . the sweet goal to clear . . . It all loomed closer and closer.

He saw that he might not make it.

The edge. The edge . . .

His body was no longer an "L." He was a fighting mass of muscle swimming in the air.

The edge . . .

His arms were over the edge. His head was over the edge. His body was almost . . .

My one leg's over! The other leg? The other leg . . .

Missed!

Down, down—the fall . . .

Would the hard barn floor beneath the loft never reach him?

The ambulance tore away from Keith's farm in a screeching howl.

"Stupid kid!" that same sneering voice screamed within him. "How come you acted so immature? So childish? So young? How come you didn't act more like a grown-up? Huh? How come, kid? How come?"

The doctor told Keith in an unattached voice, "You're going to have to wear a cast on that leg all spring."

All spring! All track season!

When Keith was in the hospital, a young woman, a school friend, visited him. God had planted a seed of love in her heart for Keith. And with the ever-athletic Keith trapped by his own mistake in a hospital bed, she had the opportunity to show him compassion. God loved Keith through her. And years after graduation they were married in Christian union. One should never tempt God, but the truth is, God has the power to grow blessings in the soil of our mistakes. Our weakness *can* be God's strength.

Wykoff's track team lost a great triple jumper. And a great triple jumper lost a shining dream. But I knew that with that loss, the world had gained a boy who would grow, in God's patient time, into a mature Christian man. Keith was a true champion because he had learned from his mistakes.

What About You?

To the world your youth is a weakness. And in a very real sense your youth *is* a weakness. But it's a glorious, wonderful weakness. It's a weakness that is really a strength because your youth is a gift from God.

Enjoy your youth. Don't let *anyone* rob you of your youth. Don't destroy your youth by trying to be an adult too soon. Childhood dies quickly. And you can't be an adult without journeying through childhood and youth first.

Yes, enjoy your youth, but don't let the foolishness of youth kill you.

To come to Jesus you must humble yourself as a child. To be forever young let Christ live His life in you.

Be young, but be wise and sin not.

"Let no one despise your youth, but set the believers an example in speech and conduct, in love, in faith, in purity" (1 Tim. 4:12, RSV).

1. In what ways do you feel society tries to make youth grow up too soon?
2. What is the difference between being childlike (the way God wants you to be) and childish?
3. What foolish mistakes have you made? What have you learned from your mistakes?
4. How can you avoid destructive actions?
5. What can you do to safeguard against growing up too fast?

6

Weakness: A Gift

A March day . . .

Somewhere, in cold and musty anticipation, the monster waited for me—crouching deep in a corner, wrapped within a dark cloak, gasping out wheezing hisses.

As I reached to open the door to the monster's room, I knew I would have to grip that cloak and pull it away. And then . . . then the face of horror would cling naked to my soul.

The room. Room 100!

But there was no monster in that room. Room 100 was filled with the young men and women I had coached for the last two years. They trusted me. And I, in turn, trusted them. Many of them had suffered with me for two seasons, and there was no reason to believe they would not suffer with me again.

So why, did I suddenly feel as if I were about to stand cringing before a gruesome monster?

Stage fright? No, public speaking was one of my strengths.

Did I feel weak because I had somehow let them down in the past? No. The people of Wykoff were positive people. They had rejoiced that Sam had competed on a state level last year, even though he had not placed.

Did I feel weak because there were new people in the room? A successful season in any sport always draws athletes to that sport the following season. Some of the new faces in Room 100 I did not know very well. Would I have to start from scratch and prove myself to these people too? Is that why I felt suddenly weak. No.

I could hear their laughter and the restless motion within the room. I had to go in.

Yes, by all rights, as an adult, a coach, and an experienced public speaker, I should be able to prance into that room and tell those "children," those "work horses," how I was going to whip them together into a championship team. Yes, I had the strength to stand firm before that monster . . .

I marched into Room 100.

The talking, the laughter, the whispering, the pinching let up as I stood before them.

"Could I have your attention?" I asked, and then . . . I saw the monster, his fangs raised, ready to claw.

Why did I feel so weak?

Adults are supposed to be stronger than kids, right? Coaches are supposed to be stronger than the athletes because they're the leaders of athletes, right? For all practical purposes, I was strong and they were weak. So why did I feel so weak?

Sometimes in the middle of our strengths, God gives us weakness. Weakness is a gift from God. But the Christian is never a weakling. The most powerful force in the universe is operating through the life of the Christian. And if Christians are not occasionally given the gift of weakness to remind them that they are "the created" and not the Creator, the strength that works through them might crush them.

My gift of weakness reminded me that I was not Superman because I was Coach. No, I was a created human being and those kids in turn were not mere athletes, to be molded into my own image. No, they too were human beings. As valuable and precious in God's sight as I am. God would never permit me to look at those young people, through the eyes of a "super coach," as statistics on paper or as "work horses."

So why do strong people sometimes feel weak when they confront weak people? Because a person given the gift of weakness as he stands before the weak will not think of himself too highly. Each of us will be reminded that we are all brothers and sisters, and there is one Father.

I looked into the faces of the star athlete. May he sometimes feel weak as he stares at the boy in the wheelchair, as waves of the latter's strength bowl him over. May that star athlete be reminded that true strength has nothing to do with muscle.

I looked into the face of the husky senior sprinter. May he sometimes feel weak as he searches the face of that sophomore girl. May that weakness remind him that she is not a plaything to be overpowered and used.

I looked into the face of the self-confident and pretty long-jumper. May she sometimes feel weak as she talks to the timid male distance runner. May that weakness remind her that the human heart is beautiful and should not be broken on purpose. May she realize that many strengths are not outwardly seen in a person.

"Track is a tough sport," I told my team. I had their attention. There was still some rustling in seats, a spit wad rolling between two fingers, a faint whispering; then all was quiet. "If you're not going to do your best; if you're not going to work the long, boring, and tough workouts; if you don't want to be a winner; if you aren't going to listen to me, then I don't think you should go out for track."

My weakness had reminded me who I really was.

"I want you to sign this sheet," I continued, "and pledge that you're going to do your best, strive to be a winner, and work hard for the next three months."

My weakness had become my strength. The monster was gone.

Everyone in Room 100 signed the pledge sheet.

What About You?

Do you sometimes feel weak when you talk to a member of the opposite sex? When you speak before a group? When you go to a school function? When you see other people?

Do you sometimes feel weak when you should feel strong?

If you answer yes to any of these, don't condemn yourself. God has given you the gift of weakness so that you will not abuse your power, so that you can see that you are no better than anyone else and no one is any better than you.

Remember, you are strong because God is strong and He lives inside you. Rejoice! Your weakness is God's strength. He will use your weakness to manifest His power.

"And I was with you in weakness and in much fear and trembling [Paul the apostle is speaking]" (1 Cor. 2:3, RSV).

1. When was the last time you felt weak facing another person? What was God trying to tell you about your relationship to that person through your weakness?
2. All leaders occasionally feel as the coach did when facing "weaker" people. What insight does this give you about leaders?
3. Can you respect someone who feels weak when he sees strength in you?
4. Do you believe that your weakness can be God's strength? What Bible passages support this?
5. God wants His strength to work through you. How can you avoid hindering His work?

7

Do You Have to Be Blind to See Clearly?

Bullets whistled all around him. But he crawled over the dead bodies, searching in vain for life somewhere. Frantically he grabbed at wrists, feeling for the pulse; he put his hand over hearts, praying to feel a steady "thump-thump" under his hand, as bombs pounded the green earth, exploding into ugly smoke, punching holes into God's creation, sending dirt clods and stones flying in all directions.

And in that mass of death and dying, there was *one* thumping heart. The medic swiftly cradled the wounded soldier in his arms, running and stumbling over the bodies as bombs exploded right and left. He gagged on the smoke. Bits of earth struck the back of his neck.

A fox hole!

He staggered as he ran with the cumbersome burden, the heavy soldier gasping out in agony, "Save me! Save me!"

The medic, with soldier in arms, leaped and dropped into the fox hole. He anxiously waited for his feet to touch the beaten earth at the bottom of that hole . . .

. . . But his feet never did.

The medic dropped the dying soldier and together they descended—down, down, into the hole. A hole that would not end. A hole that grew darker and darker. *Darker.*

"No!"

He shot up in his chair.

"This napping's getting to me," he muttered in the half seconds before coming fully awake. He thought perhaps his wife

41

would hear him, but then he remembered she was no longer there—she had been dead for seven years.

Nightmares again, he thought. *The war. So long ago. But still alive for me.*

The inside of his house was stark. Paint was peeling off the walls. Although a kindly woman cleaned it once a week, the house did not have a great deal of beauty. There were no refined works of art, no bright flowers in crystal vases.

But there was a beam of sunlight. And how Fred loved the sun. If he followed that sunbeam, he knew it would lead him to a spring day, for it was March, and the cold, sad winter was melting away.

He lifted his bent, eighty-six-year-old frame from the chair, stooped over his walker, and hobbled to his picture window.

Spring! he thought. *Melting snow. Robins. And young people running past my window! The hope and joy of youth.* His eyes penetrated into the outside.

Reed, the fastest sprinter in the district, dressed in a brand new, expensive jogging suit, his feet in the best running shoes available, stormed past Fred's window. He sprinted in the pride of being part of Wykoff's track team. His efforts last season had given his town much attention.

But running at his heels, gasping large blasts of air, moving his legs twice as fast, was a smaller and much younger boy trying to carry on a conversation.

"Hey, Reed!" he gasped out.

"What is it?" Reed responded, breathing easily, maintaining that strong runner's stride.

". . . I want to be like you . . . so I'm running like you . . ."

Reed grinned, "That's nice, Andy. Look, Coach wants me to pick up speed when I turn the corner here. I've got to go. See you in school tomorrow." Reed pumped his arms and increased his stride; his body accelerated.

"But I want to run with you!" Andy gasped out.

The distance between Andy and Reed grew, though. Andy tried to pump his arms and increase his stride. But the figure before him just kept getting smaller and smaller until Reed vanished from Andy's sight.

Andy was hobbling, coughing, trying as hard as he could to run. But he was soon walking—and very sad.

Yes, the voice that rasps out even to the very young was right there with his soiled opinion.

"Who do you think you are, kid?" it jeered. "Look at those shoes on your feet. Cheap economy specials, flapping when you run, coming apart at the seams. You don't have the shoes Reed has. And what are you running through the slush in? You don't have an expensive sweat suit. All you have are blue jeans and a jacket. You'll never be like Reed. Your family doesn't have the money Reed has. You'll never grow up to be like Reed. You're not built like him. Who are you trying to fool, kid?"

One large tear slowly traveled down the boy's cheek.

An old man looked out his window on a beautiful spring day.

He watched two people run past his window. He did not see that one had an expensive jogging suit; the other, blue jeans and jacket. He did not see that one had good running shoes; the other, old tennis shoes. He could not even see that one boy was big and the other was small, or that one was older and the other was younger.

What he *could* see were two young people running past his window. Fred had lost one eye, and the other was slowly dying. All his vision could make out were blurred images. He was legally blind.

But on that spring day, he saw two young people running in God's sunshine. What others saw as Andy's weaknesses appeared as splendid beauty for a war-torn elderly man living in a nightmare. For on that day, Fred saw two images of hopeful, happy, spring-time youth—running together in friendship.

The next day, Reed gave Andy a gift. From inside the bright wrappings and cardboard box, Andy pulled out a new pair of tennis shoes that fit perfectly.

What About You?

In no way do I wish blindness upon myself or others. But I can theoretically state that even out of a bad thing like blindness can sometimes come good. The blind person does not see all the senseless barriers that often separate one person from another.

Here's an experiment. Imagine yourself standing face-to-face with a person you don't like. Take one step backward. Take another step backward. Another. Another. Keep putting distance between you and that person until the weaknesses you don't like about him are too far away to see. It may be age, handicap, color of skin, voice, mannerisms, vocabulary, clothes, or physical features. To your surprise, you will find at a distance that the person looks a lot like you.

May you look at all people through Christ's eyes.

And remember, the very things you hate about yourself, through the strange working of God's hands, may bring joy to another hurting person.

"Judge not, that you be not judged. . . . Why do you see the speck that is in your brother's eye, but do not notice the log that is in your own eyes? . . . You hypocrite, first take the log out of your own eye, and then you will see clearly to take the speck out of your brother's eye" (Matt. 7:1, 3, 5, RSV).

1. Think about a person you don't like. What is it about him or her you don't like?
2. How many of these negative traits in that person cannot be helped?
3. How can you make yourself blind to those traits?
4. Can you think of a time when something you feel weak in, such as singing, art, speaking, or writing, brought joy to someone in a hospital or nursing home? What does this tell you about some of your weaknesses?
5. What lonely, hurting person can you visit tomorrow?

8

When Your Weakness Is a Sin

Marie was a new girl in school. I sat next to her on the bus ride to our first track meet. She told me a story of an incident in her past which displayed good and bad character.

Marie had been a student manager of another town's track team. She was a tall girl with legs too big for her body. She was in that stage of growth where she found herself stumbling over her own feet. "Awkward" could have been Marie's middle name.

She was a good student, but her awkwardness made it difficult for her to feel comfortable in social settings. Her few friends were awkward girls much like herself. They were all picked on and teased by the other girls who were less awkward.

Mollie, a sprinter, sat with two of her giggling friends on the track bus directly behind Marie. They talked about sports and boys, glorying in their popularity. They were a part of an exclusive gang in their high school. The other girls wanted to be a part of this gang, but one could not join this group unless she possessed certain traits decided on by the other girls in the gang. You had to be pretty, athletic, a rebel, or obscenely funny or you were an outsider. And if you were an "awkward" outsider, you were the object of this in-group's scorn.

"Watch this," Mollie whispered to her friend Peggy.

"Marie," Mollie asked in a mock-sweet politeness, "could you get me a roll of tape?"

Marie reached into the "meat box" for a roll of tape. But no sooner had the words tumbled out of Mollie's mouth when Peggy stated, "Marie, I need the scissors . . ."

46

But then Evie, the girl sitting on the other side of Mollie, grumbled, "C'mon, Marie, let me have some flat spikes."

Marie's face flushed; in her frustration she tried to find three things at once.

"Hey, Marie," Mollie said urgently, "I need a spike wrench—"

Marie's head shot up from the meat box. "I thought," she sputtered, "you said you needed a tape roll!" Her voice was angry—the goal the three in-girls sought to achieve. It gave them demonical delight.

"But, Marie," Mollie almost shouted. "I need a tape roll *and* a spike wrench."

"Hey, Marie," Peggy bugged, "give me some cotton—"

"It's impossible!" Marie shouted, slamming the door shut on the meat box.

At that, Mollie's hand shot out and struck the back of Marie's head with a loud smack. Peggy and Evie both burst into gleeful laughter.

Marie's eyes mirrored shock at the sudden impact. And when the pain passed out of the hollow tunnel of her soul and con-

48

nected with her face, the hurt trembling in her eyes was heart-
breaking. The pain, at last, escaped from her eyes in the form
of two tears sliding down her cheeks.

Suddenly she spun around in her seat and faced the three
girls sitting smugly on their hands looking coy, joyful at Marie's
reaction.

"Something the matter, Marie?" Mollie asked sarcastically.

"You know there is!" Marie shot back.

"What's the matter, Marie?" Peggy asked innocently. "Low
flying birds hit you in the head?" All three girls giggled in
delight.

"No," Evie said. "Not birds, jet planes." They laughed up-
roariously.

"Why are you so cruel?" Marie asked, pain returning to her
eyes. "Why do you hurt people so bad? What do you have
against—against me?"

But soon Marie realized that the more she talked the angrier she became, and the angrier she became the happier it
made the three girls. Her speech was stopped abruptly by an
ugly, inner voice piercing her hurt. "What right do you have to
talk to them like that?" the voice growled. "You're not in their
league. Look how pretty they are, how witty, how in style. Are
you any of those? Hmmm? Are you?"

Marie turned away and faced forward, looking ahead through
the rumble of the bus. A deep, hurting sigh escaped her lips as
she endured the cruel laughter behind her.

Wasn't Marie really strong to be able to live with the pain
of being abused by others for so long? She heroically made the
most of her life despite the trial of being picked on for an awkwardness she could not help. Wasn't she strong for not trying
to escape the pain by entering the horrid world of alcohol and
drugs? Wasn't Marie strong in confronting the stinging slap
with words and not fists?

In turn, weren't Mollie and her friends truly weak? With
all their strengths they still had to gang up on one person who
didn't have their strengths. And if it took three against one,
the "three" must be the weaklings; the "one," the strong.

Later, when the coach asked Mollie why she was so mean
to Marie, Mollie replied, "Oh, just a weakness of mine, I guess.
God'll forgive me if she doesn't."

What About You?

Have you ever made fun of a person, teased, picked on or tormented someone? Have you any idea the damage such actions could do?

If your sin is deliberately hurting someone, do you ever say, "Oh, that sin is my weakness. After all, I'm not God. He doesn't expect me to be Him. And didn't Jesus die for my sins? I'll just continue sinning this way and Christ's blood will wash away my sin . . ."?

Such thinking is from hell itself.

Yes, God uses our weaknesses and turns them into His strength. But if your weakness is sin, never glorify or justify it. Put your sin on the cross where it belongs by turning to God for forgiveness through Christ.

"But if, in our endeavor to be justified in Christ, we ourselves were found to be sinners, is Christ then an agent of sin? Certainly not!" (Gal. 2:17, RSV).

1. Whom do you pick on?
2. In what ways can you tell that person you are sorry?
3. What damage can be done by picking on another person?
4. Is there any known sin in your life that you will not turn over to Christ?
5. What can you do to build people up and not tear them down?

9

Recognition That Really Counts

He was the fastest man in the district. His name shone brightly on the track trophy in our trophy case as District Champion in the 100 meter dash.

Next to that trophy stood a wooden board proudly displaying all our track records. And there were two records on that board that Reed, the fastest man in the district, wanted desperately to break. The 100 and 200 meter dashes that had held firm for almost twenty years.

The times on board for the 100 and the 200 were so fast that some people felt they would never be broken. These showcase records of speed had been achieved by two young men almost two decades ago, when Wykoff didn't even have its rugged clay track. The records had been set on grass.

I've got to break those records before I graduate, Reed thought with determination.

And determination he had.

His track was mud, coarse, not pretty, but strong. His team was small, struggling to stay a team, but a team of courage. The determination, the track that forced him to be tough, and the team—all mixed together might enable Reed to turn his dream into reality.

But staring back at him from the trophy case were the ghosts of the men who had set two records twenty years ago.

The meet at Elgin-Millville. The first meet of the season.

Gun blast! The 100 meter dash!

Reed exploded out of the blocks. Almost from the start he

was in the lead. His powerful legs pumping and his arms in that odd swinging style caused the other sprinters to panic. Reed zoomed into the future, ahead, sprinting toward the tape. Beyond the tape was a dream; his name on a board in a trophy case. Reed moved faster and faster, his hair blowing in the wind.

Twenty years from now, he thought, *when I watch my children play basketball, will I walk past the trophy case and see my name on the board and hear people say, "Naw, those records will never be broken"?*

But then a lying voice weaseled into Reed's mind. "You're not good enough to break those records. And you'll be noticed by the world only if you break those records. You're weak if you don't have fame."

His spikes dug into the track. His breaths stabbed out, rushing deep from within his lungs. His face creased in strain as he heard the shouting of his team and coach storming his ears.

The thunder of approaching feet struck the earth behind him—ever near, ever close, as the haunting ghosts of never-to-be-broken records. Reed leaned for the tape.

And one record fell off the board forever.

"Unbelievable!" Elgin-Millville's coach exclaimed. Then he asked me, "Where did you get those sprinters?"

The gunshot pierced the sky again, signifying the start of the 200 meter dash. Savage feet pounded the earth, breaths raged. Eyes were dead set on winning.

The smoke cleared, the race was over. He'd won! The glorious moment belonged to Reed. His name shone in Minnesota track history as the region's best in the 100 and 200. He consulted newspapers from all over Minnesota and Wisconsin and he could not find a time faster than his own.

Yes, it had taken him two years, but on that one day, two twenty-year records were cast off the board into oblivion.

What About You?

Do you spend a great deal of time and energy trying to get your name in a "trophy case"? Do you seek fame or recognition so that you can feel special, rising above the hum-drum masses of ordinary humanity? Perhaps deep down you feel as though you have to do something spectacular before God will even notice you. If you don't have fame, does that mean you are weak?

No. Names in a trophy case are the means by which the world acknowledges strength and accomplishments. But God has other ways. There's always a younger, stronger runner hammering at your feet who will one day break your record and shatter your accomplishments. And with time, record boards will rot and fall apart.

Yes, do your best in the task at hand. Struggle to achieve and strive to be a winner. But if that record, that trophy, that "A," that part in the play, that club membership, or that job has passed you by, don't wallow in these shortcomings, giving attention to your own sense of weakness. Instead, turn to the God who loves you. The God who notices you so much that He always calls you "special" and "champion." Explore His definitions of success and strength.

"Woe to you, when all men speak well of you" (Luke 6:26, RSV).

1. What have you done in your life to receive recognition? Have these accomplishments been good or bad?
2. What do you have to do to have God recognize you?
3. What are some of the things that look like weakness and failure in the eyes of the world but are actually strength in God's eyes?
4. Does fame bring happiness? Does it guarantee happiness?
5. What can you do to learn more about God's ideas of Christian accomplishment and recognition and find out how special you are to Him?

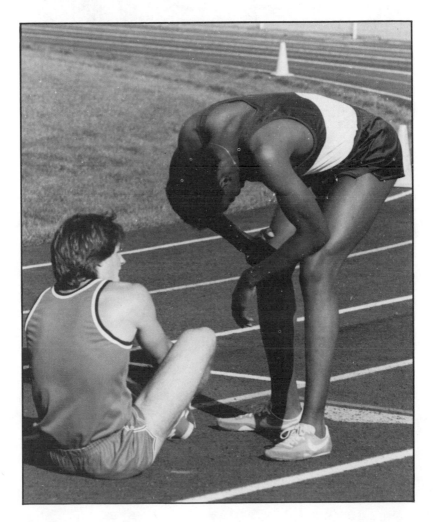

10

Glory Without Work, Ain't It Great?

Crrrack! Gunshot!

The first runner dived out of the blocks. In the opening few strides he was already ahead of the others.

He gripped the baton tightly, arms pumping, legs churning, his feet eating up the dark pavement beneath him. He crashed forward, stretching the distance between himself and the other lead-off runners.

I was amazed as I watched this opposing 400 meter relay team beat mine.

The first leg was extremely swift. The lead runner was fast, but by no means the fastest in the district. But he had worked very hard in practices and had the will to win.

He stretched forth his arm as he spotted the second runner in the lane before him. The baton hand-off was crisp. Spikes stabbed the track all around him. Grunts and gasps issued out of lungs. Then he hooked his hands on his waist, breathing heavily as his eyes stared at the runner to whom he had just handed off, watching him maintain that powerful lead.

The second runner blasted forward. Running bravely, confidently because he had worked hard for weeks and weeks, practicing sprinting exercises over and over again. On many mornings he was so stiff and sore that he could barely roll out of bed. But despite the pain, he continued to labor hard for the glory of victory. As his feet beat the earth and the silver baton glistened in the sun, he knew his reward was soon coming. He could see Lyle in the lane before him, eager to snatch the baton and carry on for the third leg.

Lyle.

"C'mon, Coach," Lyle had said days before. "Please let me run in the 400 relay."

"You're fast," the coach said, "but you're not the fastest on the team."

"Neither are the other four that want to run it."

"But, Lyle," the coach smiled, "those other four have worked very, very hard. They have never missed a practice. You have hardly shown up for one these last two weeks. And when you've been here, you've done a lot of horsing around. Do you feel you deserve to run that 400 relay?"

Silence.

But because of the illness of a sprinter, Lyle's wish became reality.

. . . The baton smacked into Lyle's right palm. He grabbed it and shot forward, running as fast as he possibly could.

Lyle enjoyed running third leg. If the first two runners established a good lead, Lyle's natural speed could maintain the lead because he ran against other third-leg runners who were usually the weakest members of their relay teams.

Lyle did not mind being in the spot reserved for the weakest runner. As a third-leg runner he could rest on the shoulders of the two hard working sprinters who ran before him. As long as the other three team members worked at practices, Lyle didn't need to work. He didn't even need to show up at practice. Because of the other three, Lyle could share in the cheers, the ribbons, and the glory.

Lyle pumped his arms and churned his legs with all his might, but the others were gaining on him. Spurred on by cheers from the girls in the bleachers, he ran swiftly. His lead was slender, but still a lead.

Cheers! he thought. *Love it. There's Ollie! Waiting for me. Here's the baton. Take it! Got it? I'll let go. And there he goes! Glory without work. Glory without work!*

Ollie's powerful muscles sprinted for the tape.

Lyle began to curse; Ollie was fighting for first place with two others.

"C'mon, Ollie!" Lyle screamed out in a rasping voice. "Beat Wykoff!"

Now it was between Ollie and our Pete. A neck and neck battle.

Spikes tore into the track. Batons flashed like combat swords.

Even! Ollie and Pete were dead even. But Ollie leaned, stretching out with his chest . . .

. . . And broke the tape. The winner!

Lyle jumped up in ecstasy. He dashed for the finish line and all four members of his relay team hugged one another.

A sinister voice whispered deep within him, "Glory without work. Ain't it great?" Then he remembered his coach's words, "They never missed a practice."

What About You?

Do you ever exploit your strengths?

Do you do your work in a mediocre, halfhearted attempt, saying, "Oh, well, if I hold back a little from being a good son or daughter, a good employee, a good citizen, a good neighbor, a good friend, or a good student, I can rest on God's shoulders and He'll pick up the slack"?

When you run in the "relays" of life, don't skip out on practice. Run like the others. Never miss a practice. Glory *with* work is great.

"Whatever your task, work heartily, as serving the Lord and not men, knowing that from the Lord you will receive the inheritance as your reward; you are serving the Lord Christ" (Col. 3:23–24, RSV).

1. What do you think of Lyle? Have you ever been like him?
2. How can you separate doing a task for the praise of humans and doing a task for the praise of God?
3. Do you feel the other runners enjoyed the victory more than Lyle did? Why or why not?
4. Are you being lazy if you let Christ do God's work in and through you? What does the Bible say about this?
5. How will you know when you are working at a task heartily, serving the Lord?

11

Even When You Don't Feel Like It

"Please, please, *please,*" she begged. "Don't make me run the 800!"

"Is your leg hurting?" I asked.

"No," she smiled.

"Any part of your body hurting?"

"No."

"You sick?"

"No, but I will be after that race."

"You're running it."

"You're a real prince," she teased. Then, half jokingly, she put her hands together and got down on one knee. "Please don't make me run the 800," she pleaded. "Get me out of it, just for today. I promise you that I'll run it next meet, and at the next meet after that. *Please* don't make me run it today."

"Look, Ruthie," I said, "you're the only 800 meter runner I have. If you don't run, Wykoff won't be represented in that event. We're small but I'd like to show our competitors that we're big enough to have at least one athlete in every event. Ruthie, we're not just a bunch of individuals; we're a team."

"I understand that, Coach," Ruth said, "and I don't want to drop out of the team. I just don't want to run today."

"Ruthie, I'm glad that if we disagree, we can at least get together like this and talk about it."

"Good." Her face lit up. "Does this mean I don't have to run the 800?"

"No. You're running it."

She laughed with faint dread upon her face. "But, Coach," she said, "there are other girls on the team who are so much better than I am. I know I'll lose."

"Ruthie," I said, "I want you to run today because I know you will do your best against tough odds . . ."

Gunshot!

The eight girls leaped from the starting line and pounded the earth. Their faces strained in the truth that two grueling laps stood before them.

Ruthie's footsteps hit the track. Step by step she fought her way to the front of the pack. She led for a while, dropped to second place, and then, showing the pain of a distance runner, she regained the lead.

When she finished the first lap, pain was squeezing in on both sides of her face.

"I'm proud of you, Ruthie!" I called out. "Just one more lap!"

She battled on in first place, struggling, fighting, but maintaining.

Then, a blurred figure dashed at her right. Ruthie was now

in second place. Soon another hazy figure flashed past her. Ruthie was in third place . . .

. . . Her fingernails dug into the palms of her hands. All her energy was fished out of a deep well within her and sent into every muscle of her body.

But another girl sped past her. Then another. Another.

She put all of her body into that race. Her mind screamed at her muscles: "Move! Move!" But those muscles were too tired to listen. Another girl shot past her . . .

"Why go on?" a voice despaired within her. "You'll get no points for your team now. No letter points. Nothing. You're too weak."

Ruthie hobbled around the last turn, suffering with an aching side. Her throat dry, she craved water. Her desire was like an Olympic champion's. But the God who had created her in His wisdom had not placed the physical force within her to accommodate that superhuman desire. Her body had gone beyond its limit of speed for such a distance.

She could have stopped and she could have dropped out. Instead, she crossed the finish line, her head held high—not in last place, but near to last. No shame.

Soon there would be a smile on her face. Her race was over.

What About You?

You may not want to visit the elderly woman at the rest home because that home's surroundings may depress you. But God is calling you to visit her, so die to your feelings, visit her, and you will discover a great secret about life.

You may not feel like showing kindness to the one who treated you so rotten yesterday. But God is calling you to be kind to him. Die to self, be kind, and you will learn another deep secret.

You may not feel like giving your money to that needy charity, but God is calling you to give. Give, and you will not be sorry.

Your sense of weakness may tell you that you can't do something, but God will always tell you that you can. You must learn to die to your feelings, especially when your feelings tell you that you don't want to do what God calls you to do or that you are too weak to serve Him. This is part of bearing your cross.

"And he who does not take his cross and follow me is not worthy of me" (Matt. 10:38, RSV).

1. Is there something you feel God is calling you to do but you don't want to do it?
2. What would you have done if you were Ruthie? Dropped out of the race?
3. Why do you think God calls us to do things we don't want to do?
4. Deep down in your heart, do you really want to do the things God wants you to do, even though you feel you don't want to do these things? Which will you do?
5. What can you do to be accepting of the crosses that God offers you to bear?

12

Love What You Hate About Yourself

He was very small on the outside—never on the inside. The very sight of him sparked nicknames such as "Mouse" or "Squirrel." In the hallways at school and in the lunch line he took more than his share of pushing. There never seemed to be a teacher around at the right time—he was small on the outside.

He was not a sports superstar. His talents were in other departments: writing, music, drama—especially drama. But despite his lack of athletic ability, he was never afraid to go out for any sport. He took each one as a challenge. And it was in this fearlessness that he was never small on the inside.

Football. He could not run very far without stumbling, and he could not catch a pass either. So his coach stuck him in the line.

The opposing linemen rushed at *him,* mashed him into the ground, and then went on to sack the quarterback. He was considered the weak spot in the line, though not for lack of courage. He was the hole by which the opposition punched their way through. The coach had to take him out of each game.

Basketball. He was put into the game only at the very end, when his team was so far ahead or so far behind that it didn't make any difference. He had trouble making the plays go. It just wasn't smooth. He would clutch at the ball passed to him like a bullet. The times he did catch it, he would dribble a few feet and the crowd would cheer.

He'd shoot . . .

. . . But the ball would never go in.

Track. He was by no means a regional champion, but I had a place for him on my team. Yes, there was a place for Willy.

One rainy day we had a practice in the gym.

He thought I did not see, but one of the guys on the team, who did not like Willy, picked up a stray basketball and hurled it at him.

It smacked against Willy's thigh—smarting, stinging, and creating a large red blotch on his skin.

Willy squinted his eyes. Pain flooded his whole being. He hated and he hated in depth. He hated completely.

No. He did not hate the young man who flung the ball at him. Willy hated himself. For too long that lying voice had wheezed within him. And now he believed the sinister words: "Look at you! You wimp! You're little and it's the big people that triumph in your world. Look at that body of yours. It's a joke. And your face? *Yuk*."

But there was a place for Willy on our team because Willy was God's champion.

What About You?

Does that voice often wheeze within you? It always seems to speak when our weakness appears great—to us and others. That voice, and what it says about hating yourself, should be ignored. And for good reason. God is your Creator. He designed you very carefully. Yes, He *made* you. And He loves you with His whole heart.

What you hate about yourself, your weakness and lack of talent is the very part God can use the most. Simply take time to say to God, "Show me how to use the weakness I hate within me to your glory."

"But who are you, a man, to answer back to God? Will what is molded say to its molder, 'Why have you made me thus?'" (Rom. 9:20, RSV).

1. Is it possible that the very things you hate about yourself may be the Creator's gifts to you to help enrich your life? What are they? What can they become?
2. What parts of yourself were created by God, and what parts were constructed by you and other people?
3. What in you do you feel God does not like? What can you do about this?
4. Think about who you are. Now think about the fact that God has created you. How does this make you feel about yourself?
5. How can you learn to "love your neighbor, *as you love yourself*"?

13

Work! Work! Work?

The dream would not die.

It formed a major part of each waking hour. Sam *wanted* to win. He wanted to shine at the state track meet. But the only way this dream could come true was through hard work and competition.

Sam did work hard each week. And he made the most of every track meet, learning from his competition with others. As a result, this year he had won all of his hurdle races. He had no champion to chase; no, this year he *was* the champion. He was at the top and everyone was gunning for him. His undefeated status was not just in one event but two—the 110 high hurdles and the 300 meter intermediate hurdles.

"How are you doing today, Sam?" the young man asked, his voice deep and resonant.

Sam shrugged his shoulders. "All right," he said, then smiled his slow and lazy smile.

Larry, the other young man, looked down at his feet for a moment and then dug his toe into the earth. "Your race start soon?" he asked.

"Yeah. Soon," Sam responded.

Larry's body was powerfully built. He had tremendous athletic ability, and he *could* be an excellent athlete. But he did not go out for sports. As if to answer the question before it was asked, he volunteered this information.

"You're a superstar," he laughed. "But me, I'm too busy for

sports. Did you know that I'm going to buy that *El Camino* this weekend?"

Sam's jaw dropped. "You are?"

"Sure," Larry said with pride. "Everybody's been giving me a rough time. Saying that I should go out for sports, and that I should find time for choir or a part in the school play or something. They tell me that I work at my job too hard into the night and on weekends. No, I'm not out for track, but I've worked, and I've saved, and this weekend I'll be driving me an *El Camino.*"

Suddenly Sam felt a strange sense of weakness within himself. The weakness that a boy feels when he compares himself to a man. Though Sam and Larry were the same age, Larry would be driving a car this Saturday while Sam would be crashing over hurdles in the hot sun.

He's got a job, Sam thought. *A car. I'm just a schoolboy who still pedals a bike . . .*

Crrrack!

Sam looked slow getting out of the blocks, but then he always did.

His feet dug into the track. A race was before him, a dream, and a goal. He put all else out of his mind.

That first hurdle shot at him.

He stuck his leg out and glided through the air. He hit the track, one, two with his feet, on the other side. Sprinting ahead, he passed one hurdler, then another as he flew over a hurdle.

Hurdle after hurdle in that 300 meter race, he cleared with ease. As he bounded for the finish line, Sam was in first place. The crowd roared within his ears.

He snapped the tape with his chest. Many hands pounded his back. Sam smiled his slow smile.

But in the distance, Larry watched—and frowned. He felt as if he were viewing a part of his life falling out of his hands, flaming up before his eyes, and settling to the ground in ashes.

What About You?

Work is important. It's important for young people to hold jobs. Working at a job can teach you about the world ahead of you. But you can work too much.

Sometimes jobs become more important to us than God.

Remember, you will be working for most of your adult life. There are certain things that give you challenge, adventure, and happiness only in your youth. If at all possible, do not deny yourself participation in such youthful pursuits.

"Remember also your Creator in the days of your youth, before the evil days come, and the years draw nigh, when you will say, 'I have no pleasure in them' " (Eccles. 12:1, RSV).

1. Whom do you envy more, Sam or Larry?
2. What are some things you can do only in your youth?
3. What things do you desire to do now that you can't wait to do in the future?
4. How important is it to you to own a car?
5. What can you do to establish good work habits both now and in the future?

14

True Heroes Fall to Their Knees

When the autumn turned to orange, a crisp chill filled the air, and the football season arrived, Sean was not outside wearing shoulder pads or a helmet.

When snow blanketed the ground, and whistles shrieked inside warm gyms, and young men and women dribbled basketballs, Sean was not shooting a ball through the hoop.

When the air was clean in springtime, and afternoon daylight lingered on into the evening, he did not pull on spiked shoes. No, Sean did not put on a blue sweat suit and pound out lap after lap on the rugged track made of clay, as tractors hummed in nearby fields.

The gym bleachers were packed with restless exuberant young people. I stood before them as the track pep fest was about to end. I had just introduced the team. Now I was addressing the rest of Wykoff's student body.

"This year our track team is winning," I announced. "We enjoy winning. Winning is a reward for hard work and doing your best. But sometimes you do your very, very best, you work harder than you ever have before, and you still lose. It is at those times you realize that doing your best is what really counts. That's why this track team believes in doing their best, *even if they end up losing*."

The final bell rang. The pep fest was over and the students headed for their lockers. Excited talk attacked the halls. Soon locker doors were slamming, coats slung over shoulders, and books cradled beneath arms.

Sean pulled on his army jacket and tucked his many science books close to his body, the book in his coat pocket making a steady "thump, thump" against his thigh.

Sean liked what he had heard at the pep fest. To him, track sounded like a fascinating sport, and attending some track meets this season might be interesting. But that was not to be. Sean needed to do chores at home after school, so that was where he went.

No, Sean did not go out for sports. And you would not see him out driving or riding in a car to a party on Saturday night. You would not see Sean at a Homecoming dance or at the prom. But Sean always had time for church, for his family, his friends, and anyone who needed help. He had time for his schoolwork. He was an "A" student, polite and responsive to the wishes of all his teachers.

When the students cheered at pep fests, they did not cheer for Sean. Cheerleaders called out many names at football and basketball games, but they never called out his name. I patted many talented and not-so-talented trackmen on the back, but I never patted Sean's back. His name was not on the list of champions' names flashing beneath the glass of the trophy case. Some would say he had no recognition.

But that book in his coat pocket, that "thump-thumped" against his thigh as he walked, was a very important book. That book was the Bible. Sean knew the Bible inside out because he always made time for reading it. He knew how Christ's triumphal entrance into any life could transform that life into glory and splendor. So he shared the transforming life of Christ with the people of Wykoff whom he loved so dearly. For this Sean had recognition.

"You don't act like other kids. You don't go out for sports. You spend all your time doing what other kids don't do. What's wrong with you?" an ugly voice from without whispered into his mind.

But while the names of Sean's friends were hailed by cheerleaders and the crowd, cheered for heroic feats on the football field or the basketball court, Sean was far away from it all. He was on his knees, praying that those young people on the field, the court, or the track, riding in cars on Friday nights or dancing on the gym floor to loud music, might know true fulfillment, true peace, and true joy, through Jesus Christ.

A power greater than a thousand football teams worked inside Sean.

His heart was large, his love far-reaching. There were many heroes in football, basketball, and track, but he was a true hero.

What About You?

When you stand before Christ face-to-face, you won't care about the letters you have worn on your sweater, or the trophies you have won. You won't care how popular you were. But you will care about whether God used you to build His kingdom.

"His delight is not in the strength of the horse, nor his pleasure in the legs of a man; but the Lord takes pleasure in those who fear him, in those who hope in his steadfast love" (Ps. 147:10–11, RSV).

1. Would you call Sean strong or weak?
2. Do you feel that God has a different definition of "strong" than the world does? If so, what do you think God's definition is?
3. If prayer, Bible study, and evangelism are more important than athletic, financial, and social glory, then what does this make you feel about the latter three?
4. When is participating in sports or social activities bad?
5. What can you do to "delight" God?

15

Where Would You Be
Without Your Weakness?

It was ugly, rugged, and like few others.

It was a simple country clay and mud track that was part of a country high school.

You could run on Wykoff's track if it didn't rain. If it rained, you tromped in sloshy mud.

We had sponsored no home track meets last season. They were too difficult to put together. All the time spent laying chalk lines could wash away to nothing with a good rain.

But this season there was a great deal of community pride over the track team. So the people of the town got together to put on a track meet.

Months before, I had invited a school from a larger town, a "city" by Wykoff's standards, to come to our track meet. This "big city school" had accepted the invitation to compete. So we packed the track down, and prayed that it would not rain.

The day of the meet arrived. I gave our track a long look as I waited for the "big city school" to appear. Our track was by no means of professional all-weather excellence, but it was a good, presentable track. We had nothing to be ashamed of. Then I saw them. I couldn't believe it.

Just when I thought we had slapped together a track of dignity and respect, *this* had to happen. *This!* What a sight!

Dandelions.

Dandelions had sprung up between the lanes of the track!

At that moment, of course, the opposing team's bus pulled

into our parking lot. What could we do? These city athletes were used to all-weather tracks and sophisticated facilities. When those young men and women hopped off the bus, I didn't know what they expected to see, but I'm sure it wasn't dandelions.

And they laughed. But I couldn't blame them for laughing. They weren't used to dandelions growing between the lanes!

As I watched the endless string of athletes pile out of their bus, I wondered if I had made a mistake. Their team was used to asphalt; our team to dandelions.

Then the events began. Since this was a co-ed meet, both girls and boys competed. The competition was overpowering. Their girls beat ours very soundly. But the boys on both teams fought it out toe-to-toe. I thought this dandelion track meet would never end . . .

. . . Nearly everyone else on my team had gone to the showers and then home to chores. Most of the "big city" trackmen had ducked into the bus. But I was still there, and so was the opposing coach. There was one event left—the high jump. Winning or losing this track meet now rested on the high jump.

Mike had legs so thick and strong they looked like oak trees. His drive, courage, and leadership on the Wykoff track team were outstanding.

The bar stood still and passive, so high on the pegs it seemed impossible to fly over. That bar meant a win or a loss.

"When you feel yourself above the bar," I said to Mike, "stick your chin into your chest. That will make your hips raise up enough to clear the bar."

Mike bent his whole body forward. One foot was placed before the other and he rocked up on his feet. Then, those solid legs began churning. That courage, that drive, that victory flashed across his face. His feet chopped into the dandelion-sprinkled grass. His eyes were glued to the high bar in a trance-like vision. His tree legs pushing, moving, plunging, and pumping.

The bar!

He curved in his desperate sprint, speeding past the left standard, just an arm's length from the high bar. His feet dug into the earth and then fired him up into the air.

High, high, higher!

He twisted in the air. He shut his eyes and gritted his teeth, expecting his head and shoulders to smash into the bar.

Instead, he flew above the bar. Then, he felt his bottom graze the bar, and his body plunge downward.

His back smashed hard against the soft pit beneath him. But his eyes were on that bar.

The bar still rested on the pegs, but jittering, wiggling, and ready to fall. Would it?

No! It quickly settled on the pegs.

However, that same height was soon cleared by two of the "big city" jumpers. Then the impossible height of the bar went even higher.

Mike attempted to clear the bar at the new height, but he fell upon it, bending it in a zinging scream.

With a grim determination he sprinted at that bar again. He leaped up, almost cleared it, but struck the bar with his hips, sending it flying off the pegs.

His tree-trunk legs propelled him toward the bar a third time. He curved, his feet dug into the grass and then left the earth.

He twisted in the air; he was above the bar! He ground his chin into his chest and flew into the sky, landing safely in the pit. Had he made it?

No. The bar lay in the grass, next to a dandelion.

That miss cost him the high jump, and he finished third behind the competitors from the "big city."

"What do you expect?" a voice sneered within me. "Of course he didn't win. Champions aren't made on a dandelion track."

But points are points. Mike didn't get as many points for third place, but he still got points. And his third-place points added to the points gathered by his teammates in other events equaled a sum larger, just barely, than our "big city" opponents. The Wykoff boys had won the track meet!

Where would we be without our clay and mud and dandelion sprouting track?

Without our track, we would not have been known as the school "with the rugged track." There would never have been a television story on us. We would perhaps be pampered and spoiled, never saying, "We don't have the best, so we have to work with what we have."

No, without our track we would never have been tough

enough to beat that "big city" team that laughed at our track. We would not be strong without the weakness of our track.

. . . No one was left on the field. Our opponents had boarded their bus and were journeying home. Mike headed home to feed the pigs. And the dandelions reached out to the setting sun.

What About You?

Where would you be without the problem nagging you now? Could that particular problem be keeping you from something worse?

Where would you be without that strict teacher who makes you work so hard, even though many times you resent it?

Where would you be without your church, even though it seems so dull to you?

Where would you be now without your parents, who lay down rules you feel are so unreasonable?

Would you be as strong as you are now without your weaknesses?

"Who through faith . . . out of weakness were made strong" (Heb. 11:33–34, KJV).

1. Think of the single most nagging problem of your life. Has God used that problem to better your life?
2. What is the "dandelion track" embarrassment of your life? Your lack of fine clothes? Your lack of friends? Your lack of money?
3. Where would you be if you had everything you wanted? Would your life be better?
4. How come God doesn't give us everything we ask for in prayer?
5. What can you do to keep from complaining to God, and to recognize His blessings instead, even if they appear to be "third place" blessings?

16

The Real Enemy

He frantically searched the locker. They were gone! No matter how hard he looked, they were nowhere to be seen. He was devastated.

Ernie had to run in the track meet tonight without them.

He pulled on his sweat suit—first the bottoms, then the top, caping the hood over his head.

I can't run without my sweat socks, Ernie thought. *That would mean wearing my black socks. With shorts! Everyone would stare at them.*

He tried pulling the pant legs of his sweat bottoms all the way to his shoes to cover those black socks. But when the time came for him to run outside, he knew that his black socks would be on display for the whole world.

A Wykoff home track meet.

The mile.

Ernie stripped off his sweat suit. The whole universe focused on his black socks.

Why did I leave my white sweat socks at home? Why? Why?

The gunshot pierced the air.

Four long, grueling, and embarrassing laps. He felt as if he were painted green, or running in a wedding dress, or had ears the size of an elephant, with two horns sprouting from his head.

The dry throat, stabbing breaths, aching fatigue, and bug-eyed exhaustion were joys, luxuries in the far corner of each lap when he was away from the crowd. But when he jogged out of the sweet pain of isolation into the crowd of spectators, the

luxuries were transformed into a torture chamber. All eyes tore into him. All eyes laughed at him. Ernie and his black socks.

She was in that crowd. Betsy. She saw his legs shining white in contrast to the black socks.

He ran his best race ever, because, on each lap, no matter how tired he was, he sprinted past the crowd.

The race was over. If the spectators noticed his black socks at all, they forgot about them within minutes of the meet's completion.

But Ernie could not forget his black socks. And he could not forget Betsy.

The next day he saw her standing by her locker at school. She smiled at him.

She's smirking at me, he thought. *Why? I remembered my sweat socks today.*

He spotted her talking to some of her friends. Soon Betsy and her four girlfriends were all laughing.

She's telling them I ran in black socks when everybody else ran in white socks, he thought. *That's not fair! The other girls weren't at the meet. Why do they need to know?*

In chemistry she usually sat next to him. But today she was on the far side of the room.

She must think I'm wearing the same socks I ran in yesterday.

He wore white socks at every meet for the rest of the season. But she never attended another meet.

She must really dislike me.

That summer he saw her downtown one day with another girl. She smiled when he walked past her in front of the State Bank.

She's laughing at me.

"Hi, Ernie!" Betsy greeted.

There's sarcasm in that "hi." I'll ignore her.

He could not sleep nights. All he could think of was how she must be plotting to hurt him. He didn't dare ride past her two-story white house with the brick front and black shutters when he'd pedal his bike home from Economy Grocery Store or Ed's Museum or Esther's General Store.

Fall.

Homecoming week. It was "Girls Ask Boys Out Day." Another school day was over. Ernie walked through the back door into the kitchen. The wall phone rang.

"Hello?"

"Ernie?" a girl's voice.

"Yes?"

"Ernie, I'd like to take you down to the Rec Center tonight. I can pick you up at 7:00. Okay?"

She's holding back the laughter, he thought. *This is a prank. Her friends are probably listening on another phone. Why does she hurt me so much? I hate her!*

"Ernie?"

"You have no class. Leave me alone!"

He slammed the receiver down.

Dial tone.

She ran into her bedroom and buried her face in a stuffed animal. She wept. Betsy could not understand why the boy she liked so much wanted nothing to do with her.

What About You?

When you dislike, fear, or hate a person, you don't usually feel that way about the real person. You dislike, fear, or hate your *invention* of who you think that person is.

People aren't our real enemies.

"For we wrestle not against flesh and blood, but against principalities, against powers, against the rulers of the darkness of this world, against spiritual wickedness in high places" (Eph. 6:12, KJV).

1. Think of a person you dislike. Do you really dislike that person or do you dislike your invention of who you think that person is?
2. Why did Ernie's dislike for Betsy get out of hand?
3. Do you believe in a devil?
4. Does this story help you better understand the above Bible passage?
5. How can you win the wrestling match against the "rulers of the darkness of this world"?

17

Mere Opinions

Distance running is an agonizing pursuit.

Running mile after mile every night is a very lonely activity. You can run with a friend, yes, but there comes a time, as you trudge out each hour of practice, when you have to withdraw and take loneliness on as your demanding companion. You have to experience the dry throat alone. And bark out the rasping breaths alone. You have to carry that stabbing sideache alone. And you have to face the plagues of shin splints, tendonitis, pulled muscles, and blisters—*alone.*

There is *drama* and *excitement* in distance running. The spectator can watch the fascinating combat between minds and bodies. But the two-mile run comes so late in a meet that hardly anyone is left to watch it, just teammates and coaches. No cheerleaders. No glory.

In the two-mile run I have seen many distance runners faint and vomit at the finish line. I've even seen some carried off the field.

Not many Wykoff athletes wanted to run the two-mile. But Phil did. Phil was only in the seventh grade. In a small school like ours, the seventh graders had to compete against the seniors of other teams. Running beside the long legs of the seniors, Phil's short legs made his age most evident. He would chase after those seniors in the long two-mile run. His short legs would blur before my eyes as I watched him try to keep an even pace with the giant strides of the other runners.

The starter fired his gun.

Phil was off with the other two-milers.

Eight laps glared in his face. But he fought with a brave heart to hang close to the leaders. One lap fell away at his feet. There were seven more cruel laps to be hammered out in pain. And now Phil battled just to stay in the middle of the pack.

His face was firm, set in determination. His tiny legs moved in strength. His feet thumped hard upon the earth.

Another lap dropped behind him, and he now faced six more.

"Crazy! What good is this?" a voice screamed within him. "Why go on? What are you going to get out of this? No letter points. No cheers. No glory. Fool!"

But he trudged on. Phil reached down, deep inside, and pulled out an energy that a true champion can always find. And he pumped that energy into himself. His eyes focused on the back of the runner who was far ahead of him. That back got smaller and smaller.

Five more laps.

Pain! Sideache! That harsh nagging agony.

"Loosen up your hands, Phil."

What was that? he thought. *My name? Someone cares?*

But that voice fell behind him with each step.

Whose voice was that?

"Don't make fists!"

The coach! The coach is watching me. Shouting for me!

Phil unclenched his fists and let his hands hang loose. The sideache went away. But soon his head was spinning. Flashing rockets fired past his right. One! Two! Three! Four! When his head cleared he realized those rockets were other runners.

Four laps . . . now three laps! His mouth was dry. His breaths were painful gasps.

Two more laps!

Last place. So far behind the man in front of him!

Quit . . .

. . . Phil felt like walking. But he did not walk. Instead, his feet tore into the track. The thumping of his track shoes hammered within his brain. His eyes were straight ahead—glued to the faraway back of the runner before him.

Fight! Reach! Pull! Pound! Run! Don't walk. Don't quit. Run! Run!

"Quit. You call *this* fun? Running is for fools . . ."

One more lap. I can see his back; it's growing smaller!
Pound! Pound!
Now his back's bigger! Bigger. Gasp. Pain!
Spit's dribbling down my chin. His back's getting bigger.
Bigger! BIGGER.

No more back! I'm at his side! He's BEHIND ME! Behind
me! Behind me. Behind . . .

. . . The race was over. Phil, the seventh grader was not in
last place. But not winning first place does *not* make you a loser.

"Bet that's the last time you're running that killer race,
right?" a teammate asked Phil on the bus ride home.

A large, open smile stretched across Phil's face. "It was fun!"
he beamed in a pure sincerity. "Can't wait to run it again." He
turned away from his friend and called across the bus to me,
"Hey, Coach! Next meet, can I run the mile *and* the two-mile,
too?"

What About You?

Other people thought the two-mile run was an agonizing experience. To them, nothing was good about the two-mile. But their opinions were just that—mere opinions. Phil managed, despite the pain, to discover good things about the two-mile.

If someone calls you weak and ineffectual, even if he calls you a "wimp," look at yourself as Phil did with the two-mile and see the truth.

God, through Christ's death and resurrection, calls you strong, effective, and a winner in His Kingdom. You are not a wimp; you are a champion.

Others may say that life in Christ is boring and worthless. But that is simply another opinion. The truth of God's Word is that the Christ life is high adventure, the most exciting life of all.

Don't build your life on other people's opinions. Build your life on the "Way, the Truth, and the Life."

"How long will you go limping with two different opinions? If the Lord is God, follow him" (1 Kings 18:21, RSV).

1. What is one "mere opinion" of other people that you consider fact?
2. What do you feel is God's opinion of you? Check your Bible for clues.
3. Do you try to please other people more than you try to please God?
4. Are you a slave to other people's opinions?
5. What can you do to ignore the opinions of people and follow Christ?

18

Walking Away Takes Real Strength

Mart was very tall and lean. Born into a farm family, he was practical and down-to-earth.

Strength was a part of him even though he seemed to deny it constantly. Strength lived deep within him, ready to be manifested when needed.

Mart did not like fights. And sometimes he endured tyrannical abuse before he would say, "Enough is enough," and fight back. Yes, he did have a temper, and his enemies feared him.

Mart was a good distance runner who could grind out mile after mile to rid himself of frustration. When it came to competition, he wished there were more distance relays. He enjoyed carrying the baton in the half-mile leg of the sprint medley relay and the quarter-mile leg of the mile relay.

In addition to sports, Mart was a counselor at a camp every summer.

One muggy summer day Mart ducked into the camp's chapel for a break from his duties as lifeguard. The chapel was a beautiful house of worship, built brick-by-brick through the monetary and physical sacrifice of the church members who supported the camp.

On this particular day, Mart had done a great deal of disciplining. Both boys and girls seemed unusually wound-up, uncooperative, and disrespectful. Now, Mart was not afraid of disciplining, but he thought it best that he get away from children for a while.

On that summer day in the chapel, a girl about twelve stood

before him, a gleam of bedevilment shooting out her eyes. Behind her were four other girls.

She opened her mouth, "Say, Mart," she began. "Did you . . ." A stream of foul language gushed out of her mouth. No four-letter words, but the intent of this mocking profanity bled with a twisted ugliness.

The shock that she had said such words under the roof of a chapel registered on the faces of the other girls. Their jaws dropped, but they could not contain their childish giggling.

Mart stood still, his heart deeply wounded, his face torn by the wicked glint in her eye.

Such words sneered at him in the past caused his anger to erupt. But he knew that anger not guided by God became personal vengence. He also knew that he needed to do *something*.

What should I do? he thought.

What will he do? the insulting girl thought, anxiety crawling up her spine.

What will he do? the other girls thought as they giggled in shame.

What should he do?

Suddenly, silently, he turned his back on the girls, walked out of the chapel, tromped down the front steps, and stormed to a big oak tree, dropping to the ground to sit and brood under that tree.

The giggles within the chapel soon turned to silence, but Mart heard a loud and condemning voice in his soul.

"You coward!" the voice mocked. "You let a little girl tear you to pieces. She humiliated you. And she was profane in a church. A little girl is batting a big guy like you around. You can't let her get away with this no matter how weak God lets you feel. You've got to stand up and protect your dignity and clamp down on her before she goes around hurting the other campers."

He sat underneath the oak tree, dumbfounded, unable to explain why he had walked away from a girl who needed to be disciplined.

That evening when the children of his cabin were brushing their teeth and getting ready for bed, Mart went running to release his frustration.

His feet struck the earth, beating at a hated weakness within himself. His long legs stretched out far distances, reaching out before him, reaching into a new life. Running, running, until his brain was numb.

Mart continued running through the fall, the winter, and the spring—all the while beating the weakness, or at least trying to.

Then Mart found the courage to tell me the whole story.

As soon as it was out, he wanted to pull back what he had told me as if he were standing naked before my eyes. "I think maybe because she wasn't too much younger than I," he said. "She was still a kid, though; but ten years from now she could be close enough to my age to marry me. I can discipline boys all right, but girls I've always had trouble with. Anyway, she walked all over me."

"You're not going to believe this," I responded. "A very similar thing happened to me once."

"That's hard to believe," Mart stated.

"We have a lot in common, Mart," I continued.

"You walked away from a foul-mouthed little girl who insulted you, instead of disciplining her?" Mart asked.

"No," I explained. "I walked away *to* discipline her. To discipline means to teach."

"I want to hear more about this."

"I just turned my back and walked away from her," I said. "Now, I don't think God always wants us to 'turn the other cheek' in a situation like this. Most of the time He probably would have us speak loving but firm words of rebuke to such 'little girls.' No, when we make a mistake, we should never try to make it holy, nor should we try to make our weaknesses holy either. But you have to remember that in dealing with people, as we let Christ live His life in and through us, approaches will vary. I felt like walking away from her after she insulted me, so by faith I trusted that God inspired such a feeling.

"I knew I had dedicated my life to Christ. And I believed that if I had given my life, my day, and my hour to God, then I could at the very least trust that the Christ who lives inside me was inspiring my actions, as long as my actions were in line with His Word, and not deliberate sins."

"But isn't that pretty reckless?" Mart asked. "How do you know for sure that God guided your actions? Maybe you were just sloughing off your responsibility of disciplining her."

"I believe God guided me because of the practical results that 'turning the other cheek' produced. Turning the other cheek can be a knock-out punch. When you don't fight back, the person who hit you feels the full pain of striking your cheekbone. When you don't take revenge against him, he can't justify the action of hitting you in the first place. All he can do is brood about the foolishness of his actions. And while he's brooding, the Holy Spirit can convict him of sin.

"In all my years of professional youth work, that girl is the only one who talked to me in such a way. But within five minutes of insulting me, she was sincerely apologizing. I never had any trouble with her again. And she grew up to be a fine young lady. So, Mart, there's more than one way of disciplining."

"But the girl who insulted *me* never apologized," Mart said regretfully.

Summer again.

Mart sat by the river with his tent group of sixth-grade boys around a noontime campfire.

Suddenly, Sig burst into their campsite with a girl doubled over in pain.

"Mart!" Sig blurted out. "Julie here is real sick! Food poisoning, I think. We have to get her to the lodge quick, but the bridge is out downstream. How can we cross the river?"

Mart studied the wretching girl. Her pain was mirrored in his face.

Mart knew of a place where some old logs nearly formed a bridge. It was their only chance:

Soon his long, angular body stretched across the powerful river, his hands gripping a log on the far side while his legs hooked onto a large branch of a fallen tree on the near side.

Sig swam across the river. But the girl crawled above the torrents, on top of Mart. She literally "walked all over him" to get safely to the shore on the other side.

Mart had been a living bridge for a girl who could not swim.

He crawled back onto the branch of the fallen tree and turned his gaze to the other side. His eyes stretched across the roaring river, staring at the young girl doubled over in pain.

He finally recognized her. The *girl of last summer!* Julie raised her head.

"Thank you! Thank you so much!" she cried in a mixture of agony and *shame.*

Then he heard it. It wasn't too loud, but Mart still heard it. "I'm sorry, Mart," the girl said.

What About You?

Do weaker people ever abuse their weakness to hurt you? Does that tiny girl playing in her front yard ever hurl insults at you as you walk past her house?

Does that old man in the rest home ever curse at you for no apparent reason?

Does that person physically smaller than you ever compensate for smallness by verbally bullying you?

Has a person who is handicapped in ways you are not ever tongue-lashed you?

I trust that in all these cases, you did not abuse your advantage of age, size, health, position or strength to "walk all over" these people.

If you have simply walked away from such people, "turned the other cheek" so to speak, then don't condemn yourself, don't wallow in guilt because you feel weak and not strong. Instead, if Christ does live in you, trust that He has guided your "walking away" and your "turning the other cheek" and your "suffering wrong instead of doing wrong."

Such a trust will produce a strength more powerful than a nuclear bomb.

"If any one strikes you on the right cheek, turn to him the other also" (Matt. 5:39, RSV).

1. Have you ever abused your strength?
2. Would Julie have apologized to Mart had he fought back?
3. How can you be a "living bridge" by letting someone "walk all over you"?
4. Can you think of situations where you should not "turn the other cheek"? Did Jesus always "turn the other cheek"?
5. In what ways can God guide you to be a "bridge of strength" for other people?

19

How Weak Do You Feel?

"I am pleased to announce that the Wykoff Track Team has just defeated a very good team."

I could not believe it. I was actually telling the people of Wykoff that my boys had defeated, if only by a couple of points, a school whose very name stood for athletic excellence.

The gym was packed with people. It was Awards Night. The milking finished, the country mothers and fathers had dressed up in their best clothes and driven into town to watch their sons and daughters receive their awards. The awards were for excellence in scholastics, music, speech, drama, community service, and sports.

I enjoyed this evening every year because it exemplified the fact that one could be a champion in something other than athletics.

The loud applause was a delight in my ears. When at last the clapping died down, I went on, "This year we've known what it's like to win. In fact, at the end of most meets this season, we found ourselves ahead of many teams—all from schools much larger than our own. Here are some of those schools." Then, I read aloud the long list. Schools that were known as athletic powerhouses. Schools that seemed as massive cities compared to tiny Wykoff.

My mind took me back two years. I was a rookie coach, inexperienced, struggling through my first season.

I was talking to Goldie in the locker room before practice. He was a quarter-miler with a distinct crop of blond hair. And he asked me, "Did you see Bob and Sarah in the hall?"

"Yeah," I said. "Looks like they're having quite a fight."

"That's not a fight," Goldie said. "That's how they talk to each other when they get along. You should see them when they're mad at each other."

The door squeaked. Bob came storming into our locker room. Our conversation was silenced. I looked at Bob and could see the extreme pain on his face.

The hood of Bob's sweat suit was soon draped over his head. He ran in the late March showers. Step after step in his three-mile run, he attempted to separate himself from the pain. He fought the realization that he could not separate his heart from his girlfriend, Sarah.

Now, years later, thoughts of him filled my mind, then pounded my brain as his feet once pounded the pavement.

For Bob would run a one-mile square day after day around Wykoff. He would run it three times a night, splashing through the mud puddles. Pushing himself hard, he would sweat and strain.

At meets, when the starting pistol would fire, Bob would crash through lap after lap of the mile run. Strong, brave, but always losing, for he was on a team of losers.

My runners of the past were losers in statistics, but champions of the spirit. Weak in team size and practice facilities, but strong in hopes, dreams, and courage.

Sunshine broke through the clouds on that rainy March day. Bob sprinted in a straightaway bringing his school into view in the distance. He imagined he was running the mile in the state track meet, fighting it out in third place, the crowd cheering.

Bob kicked it in, his body strained together in one unified movement toward the line. He could hear the cheering crowd.

He passed one runner. *Faster, yes, faster*. He passed another!

He was in the lead! He bathed in the crowd's cheers because *she* was in the crowd. Yes, his girlfriend was cheering for him— only for him.

He ran up the front steps into an empty school.

Now, two years later I stood in that school, and I told the people of Wykoff that my team was no longer a losing team. As

I read the list of over thirty schools we had defeated, I glanced at the bleachers where Sunday-dressed people were restless and sweaty, but attentive, on this warm spring night. In the past I always had to say, "Winning isn't always first place," but now I was glad that our weaknesses of size, track, and history were transformed into what we wanted them to be—strengths. Now, at last, we were *winners*!

"Aren't you glad you no longer have *losers* like Bob," some ugly and foul voice shot into my mind.

No. We were strong now because of *heroes* like Bob. We built our strength on his tears, his sweat, and his heartache. Losing does not make a person a loser.

I came to the end of the list of defeated schools. The applause shot out. It is so sweet to be winners.

The Awards Night was over. The people stuck their crumpled programs into their pockets and gave me firm handshakes. The superintendent invited the high school principal and me to his home. We laughed. We joked. We were sure that my boys would win the Maple Leaf Conference and that this would be our best season ever.

What About You?

The people of Wykoff had high hopes for my track team because we had fought through our weaknesses to become strong. Perhaps, however, we all failed to realize that we were strong *because* of our weaknesses.

When God calls you to do a task, the question He asks you is not, "How strong do you feel?" but rather, "How *weak* do you feel?"

If you feel strong as a public speaker, and you set out to convince people that they must accept Christ as Lord and Savior, you may be putting more faith in your ability as a speaker than in the Holy Spirit.

If you feel strong in your mind, and know the Bible inside out, you may be trying to understand God only with your intellectual power, shutting out the God who will speak to you through His Word if you trust Him in humble faith.

If you feel strong as a leader and you want to lead people to follow Christ, you may be leading people to follow you and not Christ.

If you feel too strong, God may cause you to feel weak.

"For we are glad when we are weak and you are strong. What we pray for is your improvement" (2 Cor. 13:9, RSV).

1. "Losing doesn't make a person a loser." Do you agree with that statement?
2. "Winning doesn't make a person a winner." Do you agree with that statement?
3. "When God calls you to do a task, the question He asks is not, How strong do you feel? but rather, How weak do you feel?" Do you agree with that statement?
4. How can your strengths retard your Christian growth?
5. What can you do to let Christ live through both your strengths and weaknesses?

20

You *Did* Reach Your Goal

4'10" was the girls' school high-jump record. Sherri's goal was to break that record.

"It's important to set goals," I told my team, "and it's important to work hard to achieve your goals."

As an exercise in goal-setting, I asked each one of my team members to write down on an index card two goals—long term and short term—for this season.

Sherri's long-term goal was to go to the state track meet. Her short-term goal was to break the school record in the high jump.

She leaped and sailed in the air, clearing the bar with ease when it rested at 4'8".

She sprinted with determination when that bar was set at 4'10". Her feet rocketed off the ground. Her body twisted, high in the air. But then, Sherri came crashing down on the bar.

She attempted jumping 4'10" again and again. She failed consistently. But she never gave up.

Then, one warm day, Sherri's feet carried her off the ground. She floated through the air on her back. The sun's rays flowed into her face as her eyes drank in the blue dome of the sky. In that brief soaring moment, suspended above the earth, Sherri felt as if she were in a magic land where all dreams were fulfilled. Her body dropped hard on the pit, but her imagination floated peacefully to the earth.

The sight of the bar drilled into her eyes. The bar had been set at 4'10½", and it still rested on the pegs.

But she had no school record. She cleared this height not at a Wykoff track meet, but at a summer track camp in LaCrosse, Wisconsin. So the school record was not officially broken.

School started in the fall. The leaves froze in winter. Spring arrived. It was Sherri's final season of track.

Soon she cleared 4'10", tying the school record. But could she *break* the record?

She tried, with determination, with grit, with force. Again and again her legs shot up off the ground, her body twisted in mid-air, soaring high, racing toward that land of dreams.

Spring ended. Sherri graduated. She had high jumped many, many times that spring, but she graduated without breaking the record . . . officially.

What About You?

Would you look down at Sherri, condemning her for failing to break the record?

Or would you remind her, "You *did* reach your goal." Her goal was achieved at a different time and place than she would have liked to achieve it, but nevertheless she did reach her goal.

God satisfies our deepest desires by giving us what we *really* want.

When God answers our prayers, it may not be in the way we would like. In fact, God may answer in such a different way that we may not recognize the answered prayer at all. We may waste our time moaning to God about His stinginess, or downgrading ourselves for our spiritual weakness. By doing this we miss a profound blessing filled with joy from the Giver of perfect gifts.

"Yet you say, 'The way of the Lord is not just.' Hear now, O house of Israel: Is my way not just? Is it not your ways that are not just?" (Ezek. 18:25, RSV).

1. Do you think Sherri reached her goal?
2. Are there any answered prayers in your life that you have not recognized?
3. Has God satisfied your deepest desire? Do you think He will in the future?
4. Should a Christian set goals?
5. What can you do to show your thankfulness to God despite negative circumstances?

21

You *Are* an Asset

As the discus skimmed across the sky, hurled from Don's powerful arms, our best discus man, John, stepped into the circle. He twirled his body around and flung the discus far into the air. It wobbled against the blue of the sky and crashed to the earth, not as far as the other throwers.

The shot put. Tossed with power and with force by Don. He was a sure bet to return to the regional track meet for another year.

But John, too, placed that shot put under his chin. Determination, drive, and yes, courage overflowed his face. He crouched into the power position, pivoted, and then the shot fired out of his hand. Arching to the sky, a black planet, dropping to the ground with a thud, it had to be dug out of the wet grass.

John was always there, every night, at practice. He worked hard. And he always cooperated with me. He competed at every track meet. But the Maple Leaf Conference track meet had room only for three competitors in every event. And the plain truth was that even though John had been very good for our team, his performance had not been good enough for a spot on the conference lineup. After all, I was out to build a "perfect team" to win the conference title.

I motioned John over to me.

He was about to throw the shot that rested in the couch of his strong fingers. He pushed his glasses back up his nose with one hand and dropped the shot to the ground with the other. Slowly he walked over to me.

"What is it?" he asked.

"John, I don't know how to say this. You've been such an asset to our team. It's been great having you aboard. But we just have to put Reed in your place for the conference meet."

"Okay," he said politely, but I could detect a break in his voice.

"John," I said. "You're a tremendous part of this team, but we have a chance to win the conference title this spring. Reed's record has been just a touch better than yours in the shot this year."

"Oh, I ah, understand . . . I understand."

But I looked into his face and could see deep disappointment, and yes, sorrow storming inside of him.

"Thank you, John. I'm sorry, but we have to do it this way."

"No, no, don't apologize, I understand," he said. Then he turned from me and walked with dignity back to the practice area. He picked up his shot put and resumed his workout even though as a senior it was his last one.

What About You?

The strong are not afraid to admit when they are weak.

God calls us all to do different tasks for Him. You may feel that you *must* do a specific task for God, when in actuality He has another "stronger" person in mind for that specific task.

True strength comes when you humbly step aside, and let God's chosen person do that specific task so that God's will prevails.

"There are varieties of service, but the same Lord" (1 Cor. 12:5, RSV).

1. What specific task do you think God has called you to do?
2. Is there any specific Christian task you are involved in now that you feel uncomfortable doing? Should you "step aside" and let someone else do the task, or would this be avoiding responsibility?

3. Why do so many Christians want glamorous ministries, but so few want to be missionaries in faraway countries or work in ghettoes or nursing homes?
4. Are you willing to be a "nobody" for Christ if that's what God wants?
5. What can you do to find out what God wants you to do with your life?

22

God Loves Imperfect People

The bus rumbled along, heading toward another track meet.

But this was not just any track meet. We were heading to the Conference Track Meet. And for the first time we were expected to win it.

There was very little laughter aboard the bus. Each young man and woman knew that a great deal was expected of him or her. And they all viewed this expectation with solemnity.

Gripping my clipboard, I faced my team as Kenny, our driver, watched me through the rearview mirror. I went over each event. I told each athlete what I expected of him or her. I could see anxious expressions on many of their faces.

"The boys' 400 relay team," I announced, "you're running against some tough competition. But I know that if you get your hand-offs smooth, if you think 'win,' and if you put *everything* you have into your race, Wykoff can walk away with a Maple Leaf Conference Championship. So Pete, Mike, Carey, and Reed, do your best."

All their faces were even more serious.

"It's up to you now," I said. "You're the only people who can bring home a conference trophy. This meet will *not* be easy."

They were confident as they piled off that bus. And why shouldn't they be? The people of Wykoff thought they could win. Other coaches thought they could win. Everyone on the team was in great physical condition. Each person was in just the right event. My teams had been doing well all season. In short, I thought my boys had the perfect team for the conference title. *Perfect.*

Crrack! Gunshot! The first event was on.

Pete gripped the baton. His arms were pumping. His legs chugging high while his feet stabbed the cinder track. He pounded out the swift determined footsteps needed to win the Maple Leaf. When he shot into the exchange zone, Mike had already started sprinting. Pete slapped the baton into his hand and Mike blasted forward, keeping a good pace in front of his opponents while maintaining Pete's forceful speed. He gave his all in the cheers, the shouts, and the dreams.

The best season ever!

Mike handed off to Carey. The exchange was ragged, but Carey, with a trophy gleaming in his eye, sprinted his heart out, ripping up the cinders with his spiked feet.

The baton was now in Reed's hand—the fastest man in the district; today, the fastest in the conference.

Reed fought it out with his opponents. He desired to win so badly that I thought his body would explode into a million pieces in the last stretch, before the screaming of the crowd. The victory was within his grasp . . .

The tape. . . !

"Lean, Reed!"

Who won?

It had been a cold spring day. Two of my 400 meter relay men were also throwing shot and discus. To keep warm, they both wore a tee shirt under the tank top of their uniforms. In the hustle and bustle to get from their throwing area to the start of the relay race, they both left their tee shirts on. And their tee shirts were different colors.

Walking towards me, one of the officials for the race was thumbing through the *Track and Field Rule Book*. Approaching me, he said, "Dallas, I'm sorry to have to remind you of Section 2 on Uniforms, article 2:

> In relay races (and cross-country competition) each team member shall wear the same color and design uniform (jersey and trunks). When other apparel is worn under the jersey by more than one team member (two or more), that apparel must be the same color.*

---

*Permission to quote from *The National Federation Track and Field Rule Book* was granted by the National Federation of State High School Associations.

I'm sorry to say your team has broken the rule."

So the 400 meter relay team that would help us win the Maple Leaf Conference was disqualified.

"Your 'perfect track team' has made a stupid mistake at the wrong time!" an ugly voice assaulted my spirit.

And yes, I was troubled; my perfect track team, by making an honest mistake through their ignorance of an obscure track rule, was not perfect.

The conference trophy seemed an eternity away.

What About You?

You may think you are perfect in body, but a trip to the dentist will leave you with knowledge that there are cavities in your teeth.

You may want your birthday to be perfect, and then it thunderstorms, or your boss or teacher yells at you.

You may want that date to be perfect, and then you end up spilling mustard on your clothes or saying something stupid.

You may, on your own power, try to live a sinless and perfect life. But then, despite your noble efforts, you sin.

You may have an inner image of yourself as a strong person, but then you fail at something, and your weakness haunts you.

Human beings are imperfect. God is *perfect*. God loves imperfect people. God forgives our sins, our failures through Jesus Christ.

"Jesus said to him, 'If you would be perfect, go, sell what you possess and give to the poor, and you will have treasure in heaven; and come, follow me' " (Matt. 19:21, RSV).

1. Do you think you will ever be perfect? When?
2. What do you think the above Bible passage means?
3. How do you feel about yourself when you make a mistake or display your weaknesses to someone else?
4. Do you forgive yourself easily?
5. Is there anything you need to forgive yourself for through Christ?

23

Bringing Out the Best

The pack was bunched close together, but she knew her time was *now*.

The young woman, born to be a quarter-miler, crashed out of the pack. The others pounding out that killing eternal lap were psyched out, seeing another who had enough energy at this point in the 400 to break away from the herd.

Sandy's spikes ate into the track. She flung herself past one runner. Then another. Another! Her eyes fired into the back of the lead runner from Spring Valley.

The quarter-miler from Spring Valley ran with both force and grace. She was an athlete who had won many ribbons, medals, and trophies. She had many God-given talents and she believed in winning. She was now in the lead, as usual, going into the last curve.

But who is this? she thought.

Sandy from Wykoff was sprinting at her side as the two went into the curve.

Can't be! the young woman from Spring Valley thought. *She's going to try to pass me on the curve!*

Such was the strategy I taught all my quarter-milers.

I had spoken to Sandy before the race. "Try passing her on the curve. That curve is so rough on runners that if you can be in the lead when you come out of the curve, I'll bet she'll be so tired she won't be able to catch you."

On the curve they were even. The Spring Valley runner panicked and picked up speed. But Sandy fought it out with

her even though ragged breaths shot out of her mouth and a hammer of fatigue beat down upon her.

When Sandy came out of the curve, her vision was blurred, her head spinning. Her spirit was faint and her feet like iron bars. But, she was in the lead!

The finish line in this one-lap race seemed a mile away.

The cheering stormed her ears, the blurred finish danced erratically in the far distance, and that champion from Spring Valley haunted her with heavy frantic footsteps. The champion was a sinister phantom chasing her in a dream.

Sandy's jaw dropped as she speeded down the runway, each numb leg falling upon the track. No matter how hard Sandy tried to sprint, she continued to digress to a slower, trudging pace. The footsteps behind her were now a thundering stampede. Everything seemed in slow motion. Sandy was so exhausted she thought she was going to tumble to the track.

Then, out of the corner of her eye, she spotted a flash. The champion from Spring Valley had caught up with her and was threatening to regain Sandy's lead.

But the moment Sandy spotted the champion, a fountain of energy sprouted up within her. Her face gained a new vitality. The finish line was no longer blurred. Instead, it crashed toward her in crystal clarity.

Pound! Pound! Pound! Sandy's feet struck the pavement, her eyes glued ahead. Breaths of life! Of victory!

"Hate her!" a voice screamed in Sandy's brain. "She's always beating you!"

But in a flash of revelation Sandy knew that she did not hate the champion from Spring Valley because she always defeated Sandy. Rather, Sandy loved her because she brought out the best in Sandy . . .

. . . The tape. . . !

Sandy walked off the track in second place. She carried with her no trophies or ribbons. Instead, she carried a great admiration for the victor.

What About You?

Don't hate your opponents for defeating you; love them for bringing out the best in you.

Don't hate yourself for your weakness. Realize that your weakness will cause you to drop to your knees, seeking in prayer the true strength, which is from God, the God who will bring the best out of you.

"Bless those who persecute you; bless and do not curse them" (Rom. 12:14, RSV).

1. Who are your opponents in life? Do you feel your opponents persecute you?
2. Do your opponents bring out the best in you?
3. Do your weaknesses ever cause you to seek after God?
4. Do you hate or love your opponents?
5. Do your weaknesses ever bring out the best in you?
6. What can you do to bless and not curse your opponents?

24

What is *Your* Definition of Strength?

Our 200 runner gripped the baton as his churning legs beat the track. His arms were pumping; he sprinted with a speed that surpassed all others, dashing in a glint of pain. Then he handed off to the second runner in this sprint medley relay, who fired around his half lap until the baton was in the hand of the quarter-miler who did his best to maintain the swift pace. He fought, he overpowered, he even passed a runner, and then handed off to James.

James was our 800 runner in this long relay. And he always pounded out the two laps with force and courage.

The sun beat against his dark skin, and the harsh wind slashed his black hair. The expression on his face was of a true athlete. His eyes were straight ahead, always forward, never contemplating for a moment the thought of quitting or withholding any energy that would cause him to drop back.

As he ripped into the second lap, I could see the pain eating into his face. The 800, two cruel laps in a near sprint, is a devastating race.

Pain! His breaths chopped out in a gasping agony. His heavy feet beat the track. *All out! Forward!*

James could not catch the two trackmen before him, they were just too far away. But he could stay ahead of the raging monsters of exhausted breath and spit who tortured the track immediately behind him.

Stay ahead! Stay Ahead!

And the three trackmen, their spikes sending the clods of

earth flying, trudged closer and closer. But James, in his stubborn tenacity, kept his eyes forward and crossed the line.

No, he did not win first place, but by doing his best, he gained important points for his team.

James was a vital part of Wykoff track, a conscientious addition to any coach's athletic program. But a funny thing happened at the end of this our "best season ever." James decided not to go out for track again.

Why?

James possessed a unique courage that everyone wants but

few people have. Though he continued to play football and basketball, he decided that despite what society preaches, sports was not the most important pursuit in the world. He wanted to be a champion in scholastics and music and drama, and spring was a time for plays, concerts, and final tests. Track was in the spring also, so he retired from track and field.

James did not care what sports worshipers might say about his decision. And he did not believe the foolish who claim that athletics are the only tests of strength. He had the courage to live by his own concept of strength. His strength was a strength that followed what he thought was right. He believed that the world needed athletes, yes, but he believed that the world needed scholars, musicians, and drama players even more.

James was a young man of strength, and I'm proud that he was part of our team.

What About You?

Don't listen to other people's definitions of strength, no matter how convincing their definitions may sound.

May the definition of strength that you apply to your life be the Bible's definition.

And what is the Bible's definition of strength?

The joy of the Lord.

"For this day is holy to our Lord; and do not be grieved, for the joy of the Lord is your strength" (Neh. 8:10, RSV).

1. Do you think sports holds too high a position in our society?
2. Is there anything or anyone in your life you worship more than God?
3. What does "the joy of the Lord is your strength" mean?
4. How can God's definition of strength be yours?
5. How can God's strength operate in your life?

25

Courage in Discouragement

Wykoff's boy's track team was supposed to win the conference track title. Many people expected such a victory. And just about everyone in the community hoped for such a triumph. After all, I had built the "perfect" track team. And wasn't this to be our "best season ever"?

It was the day after the Maple Leaf Conference Track Meet.

Pete walked slowly into the locker room. Sam soon trailed behind him. Then Reed blew open the door. He was followed by Mike, then Don.

Pete grimaced up at me. "Not many feel like coming to practice tonight."

Don gave a broken smile. "But *we're* here, Coach," he said.

Last night we were expected to win the conference. But Spring Valley, Grand Meadow, and Chatfield had all beaten us. *Fourth place.*

My greatest challenge as a coach now stood before me. We had lost the conference. No alibis. No excuses. On that day, even though every boy on that team ran his heart out, everything seemed to go wrong for us. Yes, there were some excellent achievements, but we still finished in fourth place. And such a fate may be the dent in our armor that would eliminate this season as "our best season ever." What I had to do now as coach was to make sure the dent in our armor didn't kill us. Despite the fact that we may have lost our chance of having our best season ever, we had to pull together and find strength in our weakness. Despite this great loss, we would go on, we would

109

triumph. No matter what our critics said, no matter what our ranking at the end of the season, we would never quit. We would continue to give our utmost. I had to lead every youngster on my team to embrace such a spirit.

"It's hard to get fired up," Reed said.

"So what!" Mike snapped. "We've got to go on."

It took them all a long time, but at last, in great labor, they pulled on their sweat suits.

The word "courage" is found in the word "discouragement."

Yes, they were discouraged, but as strength needed to be found in their weaknesses, so, too, courage needed to be found in their discouragement. Pete, Sam, Reed, Mike, and Don all marched outside, holding their heads up. They attacked the day in their long grueling workout after a *bitter* loss.

I watched the door of the locker room close that night as the last young man went home. The silent showers caused a quiet sadness within me as I picked up a stray towel off the floor.

"Don't you wish the season was over?" a sneering voice tempted my soul. "Don't you wish you could put an end to the dull ache of defeat? Wouldn't you like the motto 'Winning is always good' instead of 'Winning isn't always first place'?"

But the next day, after school, that locker-room door shot open. Sam marched into the room followed by Pete, Reed, Mike, Don, and a whole stream of others.

The night after that, more came. The next night, even more. They all merged together as a mighty army that would seek courage in their discouragement and strength in their weakness and victory in their defeat.

The whole team was soon back on our rugged track, training for the district track meet.

What About You?

The discouraged can demonstrate true courage by showing courage in their discouragement.

Your discouragements are not to be whined and whimpered about. Instead, look at your problems as golden opportunities for God to act in your life. Then you can take courage in discouragement.

"Wait on the Lord: be of good courage, and he shall strengthen thine heart; wait, I say, on the Lord" (Ps. 27:14, KJV).

1. "You have to be discouraged before you can show courage in the face of discouragement." What do you think about that statement?
2. In order for God to strengthen our hearts as the above Bible verse says, it's logical that our hearts must first be weak. What does this make you feel about weakness?
3. What insights did the story give you on "discouragement"?
4. After a defeat in your life, how do you respond?
5. If it is God who gives strength, courage, and victory, what difference should that make in your life?

26

Your Day Will Come

Why did we lose the conference track meet?

Now that the meet was over I came to the conclusion that it had been unrealistic for us to dream of winning the conference title while ignoring our size.

We were still the smallest track school in the conference.

A track team with many athletes has an advantage over a team with few. The coach of the many can pick and choose the very best. The large team's athletes can specialize in one or two events. They don't have to spread themselves so thin; they don't have to exhaust themselves by competing in four events each track meet.

Yes, our size always has been a major obstacle, but Spring Valley had a small team this year too, and they won the conference title.

Why did we lose? Everyone on my team tried with all their might to win. They were all in the right spots. We had many individual conference champions, but we still had lost.

True, many things had gone wrong for us on that conference day, but I wasn't looking for excuses. We were the losers plain and simple. Yet I was proud of all my athletes. Even though many things had gone wrong for us at the conference meet, the Wykoff track team stood tall, refused to quit, and fought for victory. Even after the defeat, they regrouped and prepared for the district meet, still believing that this could be their "best season ever."

So why did we lose? Many people asked me that question. I

could give them no simple answer. Sometimes you lose because you lose. And facing that loss with dignity and courage makes you a winner.

We *still* had many things to be proud of. Like Sam's new 14.86 school record in the 110 high hurdles—a time better than the school records of many high schools across the nation . . .

. . . Gunshot!

He fired out of the blocks. Crashing toward the first hurdle, he fought, he pushed, and he strained to stay in the lead.

Who is that moving ahead? he thought.

First hurdle!

He shot his leg forward.

Pain!

He upended the hurdle. The accident knocked him off balance. He staggered and stumbled until he was again sprinting for the next hurdle. But his steps were off. His form over the hurdle was awkward. His weak leg stuck out. Both arms reached forward, and his body slanted too far to the right.

Again he stumbled. His eyes burrowed into the track, and when his eyes were again steadied forward, he saw the other trackmen striding over the next hurdle.

He bounded toward that hurdle and leaped over it, knocking it to the pavement. By the time his feet hit the track, he was even farther behind the other hurdlers.

He staggered. He stumbled. He cleared the remaining hurdles, finishing in last place.

This youth was Wykoff's other hurdler.

On the bus ride home his teammates sang him a song:

> "We know a hurdler, his name is Craig,
> No letter jacket to hang on his peg.
> His form is great, he looks so fast,
> So why does Craig always come in last?"

The bus laughed in good fun. And with a bright smile Craig also laughed.

Sam turned around and grinned at him. "Your day will come," he said.

"Sure hope so," Craig smiled.

Sam the Champion. He had been to the state tournament and people thought this year he would be Wykoff's first regional champion. Some thought he would even win the state title.

He never stumbles, Craig thought. *He never loses his balance. He never comes in last place. His form's not like mine. His build's not like mine. His steps between the hurdles aren't the same as mine. I don't have the endurance for the intermediate hurdles that he has. I don't—*

"Craig," I told him. "Sam's a great guy for a hurdler like you to have for a hero. But don't compare yourself to him. He's a senior. You're only in the ninth grade. He's taller than you because he's older than you. He has more experience because he's been out for track longer. Sam's got a lot to give to the sport because of who he is. But you have a lot to give to track too. What you have to give will be different than what Sam has to give because you're you and Sam's Sam. Don't get down on yourself for not being Sam. Congratulate yourself for being you."

Craig smiled at me.

A year later he broke out of district and advanced on to regional competition. His team never sang him another song.

What About You?

Do you ever condemn yourself because you don't measure up to someone else?

And who is this "someone else"? What is he or she like? Do you tend to think of him or her as perfect? A god? Don't you realize that "someone else" is condemning himself because he does not measure up to another "someone else"? Your "someone else" may have great strengths, but the greater the strength the greater the weakness. And everyone is weak compared to God. It all balances out.

You have the same potential as anyone else to be God's champion, as long as you live in the will of God. Your day will come.

"But when they measure themselves by one another, and compare themselves with one another, they are without understanding" (2 Cor. 10:12, RSV).

1. Who is the "someone else" in your life?

2. Think of the statement, "the greater the strength the greater the weakness." How does that make you feel about your "someone else"?
3. Do you ever condemn yourself for not being perfect? For not being God?
4. What is the difference between trying to be God and letting God in Christ live His life in and through you?
5. What can you do to better appreciate how God made you?

27

In the Eyes of the World

"I can't believe it!" Jamie said, crumpling up the newspaper in his hands. "What's happening to those guys?"

He reached across the kitchen table, grabbed the handle of the pitcher, and poured himself a glass of orange juice.

"You what?" his elderly landlord asked from the living room as she dusted around some potted plants.

"Oh, nothing, Agnes." Jamie sighed as he sipped his orange juice and hissed out a sad breath. "I'm just worried about the Wykoff track team."

Then suddenly, his mind took him back to last year.

He had possessed the fastest sprint times in the district. When the starting pistol fired he would dive out of the blocks, his spikes spearing the track and his arms punching the wind. His lungs would shoot out bullets of air. The eyes of other runners would fill with fear as he blasted forward, faster, faster, impossible to catch, until all their eyes could see was his faraway back, supported by powerful legs, crashing across the finish line in a hazy blur of victory.

But that one race, on that cold day, oh, how he remembered it now.

Pain! Pulled muscle! Injury!

He could no longer sprint. He could shag. And he could jog. He could maybe even limp out a mile or two around the track. But he just couldn't sprint.

Jamie worked, and worked, and worked. Soon his leg was strengthened. Maybe he wouldn't be the fastest man at the

117

district track meet that year, but he would still run the 100 and 200 with dignity.

District Track Meet!

Gunshot! 100 meter dash!

Will the leg go out?

No.

"Did he win?"

No.

200 meter dash! Gunshot!

"Will Jamie's muscle pull out?"

"No!"

"Well, did he win?"

"No."

He won no medals, but his courage won points, valuable points that added to other team points helped Wykoff win the District Runner-Up Trophy.

"Will they win another trophy this year?" Agnes asked him, breaking up his reverie of the past.

"Well, they *couldn't* even win the conference," Jamie commented in his soft Alabama drawl.

He had graduated last year the captain of his football, basketball, and track teams. He had also been the president of the student council and the Homecoming king. He was an excellent student who would be going faraway to an out-of-state, four-year college. Jamie was a figure of strength.

But today was a year later.

He was living in the upstairs apartment of a farmhouse seven miles from Wykoff. He had not gone on to the four-year college. He was driving a church bus, working at a job, and taking a class here and there in a junior college.

He often wondered what his fellow classmates thought of him. He had looked so strong last year. But today he felt so weak.

Did those classmates understand that the world's strongest people often look weak in the eyes of the world?

An elderly woman needed a young companion to look out for her, and to care for her if need be. She yearned for a young face around her house to bring her joy in the twilight years of her life. Jamie would be that face.

A church bus needed a driver so that boys and girls could

attend a Sunday school aflame with the Spirit, and hear the gospel of Jesus Christ. Jamie would be that bus driver.

Money needed to be earned—honest money, through hard labor, over the patient pilgrimage of time. In his work he would learn resiliency and longsuffering; he would grow into maturity and stand tall in his manhood. Eventually, Jamie paid his way through a four-year college in Illinois, became an outstanding miler on their track team, and graduated with his head held high.

The Spirit of God would lead him into a shining future.

What About You?

The strongest people in the world often look weak, for Christ's sake, in the eyes of the world.

If you are a man, the world says that to be strong you must be insensitive, brutal, uncaring, and "macho." But for Christ's sake you will find strength only through being kind and gentle.

If you are a woman, the world says that to be strong you must boldly exhibit your physical beauty. But for Christ's sake you must let your *inner beauty* shine instead.

The world says that to be strong you must be wealthy, but for Christ's sake your life may have little to do with the wealth of the world.

The world says that to be strong you must be aggressive, learn the art of intimidation, and fight to the top in society. But for Christ's sake you are called to be humble, and your place in society may be a lowly one.

In all the "weak" tasks that God's Spirit gives you, you will realize that the Christ life is the most exciting life of all.

Do you have the courage to look weak in the eyes of the world for the sake of Christ?

"When you are invited by any one to a marriage feast, do not sit down in a place of honor . . . sit in the lowest place. . ." (Luke 14:8–10, RSV).

1. Can you think of a time when you looked weak to others as a result of your faithfulness to God?

2. Jesus Christ was the strongest person who ever walked the earth. Think of a time in which He looked weak in the eyes of the world.
3. Is it wrong for a Christian to be wealthy?
4. Read the Bible passage again. Then read Luke 14. What does that passage mean?
5. What can you do to live the life God has called you to live?

28

Chewing Out with Love

My track team was shaping up.

I stood on the infield, my eyes scanning the practice field. It seemed as if I had been doing a lot of yelling today.

"Pump your arms, Phil!" I called to the distance runner as he finished his last mile on the rugged track.

"Grind your chin into your chest, Mike!" I shouted to the high jumper who had leaped above the bar.

"Don't look behind you, girls!" I called to the athletes practicing for the relay race. "Get those handoffs down smooth."

Then my eyes searched into the far distance to the pole vault pit.

Yes, Tim had a lot of promise as a vaulter. It takes years to perfect a pole vaulter. But I could remember the end of last year's season when Tim, the seventh grader, at his first try, gripped the pole, sprinted down the runway, speared the plant box, and vaulted seven feet. His first try!

Now, a year later, Tim was vaulting higher every day. I could see him in the distance. He rocked on his feet with pole in hand. Soon he was racing down the runway, stabbing the sky with his pole. He shot closer to the plant box. Closer. Closer.

His pole jabbed the plant box.

Just then I realized I wasn't watching Tim vault at all. No, it was Reed, the man who had just won both the 100 and 200 dash championships in the conference. A sprinter. *Pole vaulting?*

Reed struggled and fought his way up in the air. And some-

how, through pure force, he horsed his way over the bar set at eight feet. And then he fell down hard on the pit.

My wrath, too, fell down hard on him.

"Reed!" I yelled, storming at him. He quickly popped to his feet. And by the time I reached him he was looking very sheepish. I proceeded to "chew him out." I expressed my disapproval in no uncertain terms. My anger was distinct, enraged, but controlled. And the majority of my track team witnessed the "chew out."

Why did I scold him? Was it because I was afraid pole vaulting would injure my best sprinter so we could not have our "best season ever"?

No. I scolded him because I cared about him.

Reed was a strong track man, but pole vaulting was not his strength. When a person treats his weakness as a strength, injuries often happen.

I didn't care if he was my fastest sprinter or my slowest sprinter; I didn't want him to get hurt.

I cared about him enough to "chew him out." If I had not voiced my disapproval over his foolish, untrained pole vaulting, he would have perhaps continued his foolish actions until he hurt himself.

After my angered and impassioned speech, Reed looked at me with tight lips. He nodded his head, and then said, "Sorry, Coach." Gratitude showed on his face.

What About You?

Following Christ may sometimes make us look weak in the eyes of the world, but other times the Spirit will lead us to look strong. Under God's strong guidance we will scold people out of love for them. If we don't voice our disapproval over sin and evil in the world, sin and evil will be justified by the world.

Christians are called to take the offensive, be combative, and "fight the good fight."

"Whoever brings back a sinner from the error of his way will save his soul from death and will cover a multitude of sins" (James 5:20, RSV).

1. "When a person treats his weakness as a strength, injuries often happen." What do you think of this statement?
2. Have you ever gotten angry at a teacher, coach, boss, or parent who scolded you?
3. Did these people show their concern for you by scolding you?
4. What is the difference between Holy Spirit controlled anger and human anger?
5. Can you think of a person you should talk to who is involved in dangerous and harmful actions?

29

We Never Know...

He walked down to the little warming house every night. His back was slightly hunched and his eyeglasses were thick. Something about his walk seemed imbalanced. His voice was gentle, his spirit mild.

Paul supervised the park's warming house. The children skated on the ice outside. But Paul was always inside. When the children got tired of the Minnesota cold and the ice and the skating, they would go inside for warmth and hot chocolate that Paul brought from home, and for entertainment, which usually consisted of teasing Paul.

The children didn't respect Paul very much. To them he didn't seem to have the strength a grown-up should have. Most of the time it appeared that he *let* the kids abuse him. Maybe it was because he was handicapped in some mysterious way, but nobody seemed to understand the nature of his handicap. He was a "soft touch," an adult to take advantage of, borrow money from and never pay back, laugh at, make fun of, swear at.

"Most of the time he just smiles at you with that stupid smile," the children would sneer. "And Paul Berden doesn't even live in this town. He lives over in Wykoff . . ."

. . . Karen was an outstanding athlete. She shined on both the volleyball and basketball teams. And she was a good sprinter and high jumper. She was attractive and popular. A true lover of the outdoors and the vigorous life. She said that one day she would climb a mountain in Oregon. Karen was also an excellent student. I was very impressed with the following paper she wrote for an English composition class.

My Hero

The man that I admire the most is a man who showed great courage in the Viet Nam War. He was a great leader of men. My problem is that I've never been able to get him to tell me what his brave actions were because he's just too modest to talk about it. From what I gathered in talking to his wife is that he rescued many men and helped many men. He even took some bullets meant for the men that he rescued. He received many medals for his bravery and even a letter from the President of the United States.

But my hero hates war. He says that he's seen too much pain and cruelty. He got a job doing piece work in a factory part time. But what he really wants is a job as a teacher. But you see, my hero is handicapped from the war. People tend to think that he couldn't function as a teacher; he'd have too much trouble disciplining. So every night of the winter he volunteers at an ice rink. He says when he looks in the eyes of every child, he sees God. So he treats them as vessels of God. But I'm sure that the children don't understand my hero and don't know that he's been in the war.

My hero says that war taught him a lot about human nature. He says that people can be cruel, but it didn't take a war to teach him that. He says that he lets the kids at the ice rink hurt him so that they don't hurt each other. There are certain kids at that rink who just plain want to hurt other kids. My hero says that he can handle that hurt more than the little children can. So he lets the older kids hurt him, and they're so busy hurting him that they don't have time to hurt other kids. His strategy works too. Before my hero started working at the rink, little girls were always going home in tears because other children insulted them. Little boys would always get beat up. But this doesn't happen anymore.

My hero says that all he has to give to the children is his smile. And I know that his smile is very sweet. He says that his smile will one day haunt the kids. They will remember how he could smile at them when they were so cruel to him. And that smile will cause them to be kind to their own children and look very close into their own children's eyes, and perhaps see God too.

My hero has the guts not to swagger in a false macho fantasy land. He has the strength to be gentle.

How did I get to know about my hero?

My hero is my father, Paul Berden.

Karen Berden
Grade 9
English Composition
Wykoff High

What About You?

We rarely *know* a person. We never really know the hard journey a person may travel through life. We never know of the deep pools of strength that may be within a person. What we sneer at as a weak reed pounded about by the force of the wind may be a roaring lion; and we, the sneerers, the weak reeds.

"Do not judge by appearances, but judge with right judgment" (John 7:24, RSV).

1. How does Paul remind you of Jesus?
2. How did Paul's weakness become a strength?
3. What were Paul's strengths?
4. How did you feel about Paul before you read Karen's composition? After?
5. How can you look on all God's people with fairness and kindness?

30

True Strength

The bus was packed, and Kenny, our jolly driver was taking us to the district track meet.

As my eyes scanned the restless conglomeration of youth, I thought back to last year. Our scrappy track team had taken home a district runner-up trophy—the first track trophy in the history of the school. And this year we thought we could do the same thing because many of those strong athletes were still a part of the team.

But things were so different this year. Most of those strong athletes were not sitting on the bus before me. Why?

The dates for the senior class trip had been planned way back in September. No one had realized that the dates picked for the trip would clash with the district track meet. And by the time it was realized, many of the senior tracksters had already paid their nonrefundable deposit to go on the trip to Minneapolis.

So what would we do?

It was a classic example of priority-setting. The senior class trip was a "last hurrah" before graduation—one final chance of fellowship for people who had grown up together.

A short time from now, some of my graduating seniors would be defending our country in the military. Others would be married. And some would be preparing for adult careers in college. It would be hypocritical of me, as one always preaching self-discipline, to treat these seniors like children.

"I know how important it is to you to take home another

trophy this year," I told my senior trackmen. "Some of you, by scoring in the top three places in your event, can advance to regional competition, and from there perhaps even to state."

"But you're about to graduate from high school as adults. I've preached responsibility for three seasons. Now *you* have to make a decision."

Some did not go on their senior class trip at all. The others left the trip from Minneapolis, and one of their parents drove them to La Crescent to compete in District on Saturday.

And now we were riding on the bus to meet them.

Obstacles had always blocked the Wykoff track team. Our size. Our track. Our inexperience. But why such an obstacle now? Why?

"What kind of kids do you have on your team anyway?" an implying voice asked.

I thought of some of those sacrificing athletes who were now in another vehicle, heading toward the district meet.

Sam.

The gunshot! He would crash in violent strength over hurdle after hurdle. Then diving across the finish line, he would remain undefeated for the season.

That same build, that same courage, those same long legs enabled Sam to leap, in an unorthodox hurdling style, over the high-jump bar. Sam's strength as a hurdler was his strength as a high jumper. He would not have been a hurdler if he had not been a high jumper.

I looked at the seniors aboard the bus who had not gone on their class trip.

Don.

When he pivoted in the circle and his pulsating muscles pushed out that heavy shot put, it ripped through the sky and tore into the earth a far distance from where he had stood when he started the throw.

That same strength, that same coordination translated into the power he used to spin around with tremendous speed and released the discus so that it pierced the sky and stabbed its way to earth. His strength as a shot putter was his strength as a discus thrower. If he were not a discus thrower he would not put the shot.

Then I looked at some of the younger people on my team.

Lynn.

She would fly across the row of 100 meter low hurdles. Then with profound endurance, her feet would beat the track and her body would skim over the hurdles again, for 200 tough meters. But her drive and will and athletic ability were also tested in the high jump. In her final event, her feet would pound the runway and leap high into the air, her legs shooting out before her; and then with her body crashing into the sand, she would win the long jump.

Lynn's strength as a hurdler was also her strength as a high jumper and long jumper. If she was not a long jumper, she would not be a high jumper or a hurdler.

The bus rambled along, heading for our destination. I knew my tough little team had the strength to take home a trophy.

What About You?

If you do not have love, joy, peace, patience, kindness, goodness, faithfulness, gentleness, and self-control, you do not have strength. These fruits of the Spirit are also attributes of God's character, and God gives true strength (Isa. 26:4). God is strong because of these fruits. If He did not have these fruits, He would not be strong.

To have God's fruits of the Spirit and strength operate in your life is a gift-like privilege from God. You cannot earn such a privilege, so ask Him for it.

"But the fruit of the Spirit is love, joy, peace, patience, kindness, goodness, faithfulness, gentleness, self-control; against such there is no law" (Gal. 5:22–23, RSV).

1. What is true strength?
2. What is true weakness?
3. Can you have strength without love?
4. Describe a strong person you know. What makes him or her strong?
5. What can you do to have the God who gives strength live in your life?

31

Victory Veiled in Weakness

The bar peaked high upon the standards against the darkened sky.

Tim had to vault over that bar with the long pole he held in his hands. Now it was his turn to vault. Wykoff depended on him.

But Tim was not the best pole vaulter in the district. He was not even the best vaulter on our team. There were two other Wykoff vaulters he considered superior to himself. Also, Tim had been vaulting only a couple of months, and it takes years to perfect a pole vaulter. Tim was only in the eighth grade. He was small compared to the lanky senior pole vaulters from other towns. Tim had been put in the line-up on this District Saturday because he was the only other vaulter from Wykoff who could vault on this day. No one expected much out of him.

The wind tousled his hair. He held the pole up, the tip just even with his eyes. He rocked slightly; then his legs shot forward. Tim dashed down the runway, the pole quivering in his hands.

There are only two vaulters from Wykoff, he thought. *I've got to do my best. My best!*

His feet thrashed the earth. His eyes tore into the high bar.

"Impossible!" an ugly voice cried from deep within him. "Who are you? An eighth grader with no experience. You're too weak!"

Pole quivering. Feet pounding. Destination: the darkened sky.

I'm just one of two, he thought. *Wykoff needs me!*

He gripped the pole tightly. His eyes dug into the plant box. *This is it . . .*

. . . Tim speared the box with the tip of his pole. He thought it would be just like swinging up the branch of the oak tree on the farm. He felt his body go up—higher and higher. The pole bent, forming a large fiberglass "U."

Will it break? Snap? What?

He felt the pole fling him upward.

Flying. Freedom. Can I?

The bar. . .

. . . *I'm above it!*

Tim fell downward in the sweet ecstasy of victory.

Plop!

Home again on earth.

But suddenly he felt an irritating sting of cold metal on the top of his head. The high bar had followed him to the pit. He had failed.

He had only one vault left.

I was deeply disappointed. After losing conference not so long ago, we weren't doing as well at this district track meet as I had anticipated. Would we send even fewer athletes to region this year than we did last year? Wasn't this supposed to be our "best season ever"?

I felt a tap on my shoulder. I turned around, and standing before me was a young man with a happy grin.

"I did it, Coach!" he beamed. "I'm going on to regions!"

"*What?*" I was dumbfounded. I hadn't expected anyone to go on to regions other than Sam and Don and Reed.

"I finished third," Tim said, with humility and a touch of shyness.

I had been more aware of Tim's weaknesses as a pole vaulter at this district track meet than I was of his strengths. But his strength had delightfully surprised me because that strength had come out of his weakness, a place where I had never expected it.

Tim's accomplishment of third place was not impressive by the world's standards of strength. But because of his weakness, his accomplishment astounded me. In fact, weakness was the darkness that let the light of his accomplishment shine. If not for his weakness, his victory would have gone unnoticed.

What About You?

A strong, verbally persuasive, professional football player suddenly becomes a Christian and is a "dynamo for the Lord," sharing what Christ has done in his life.

People say, "He's always been so dynamic. He's always spoken his mind boldly about football rules, sports writers, and even politics. Now he's using his strength to promote religion. Isn't that great?"

The neighborhood runt. Timid and always picked on. He asks Christ to live His life through him. Now the "runt" has a holy boldness. He fearlessly witnesses about the life-changing power of Jesus Christ to the bullies who once picked on him.

People say, "He's so bold. That's just not him. It has to be the Holy Spirit in him. Christ has to be real."

Our weakness is the darkness by which the light of Christ shines brighter.

"God chose what is weak in the world to shame the strong" (1 Cor. 1:27, RSV).

1. How can it be that Christ is seen clearer in human weakness?
2. Can you think of a time in which Christ was made strong in your weakness?
3. Look at the above Bible passage again. Should you hate your weakness?
4. Do you think people notice Christ working through *your* weaknesses?
5. What can you do today to enable Christ to work through your weaknesses?

32

Christmas Without the Merry

For all practical purposes, this long-awaited District Saturday was over.

We all stood before the empty bleachers. We looked up into the press box at the top of those bleachers where the statisticians were tabulating the order of the finishing teams from top to bottom.

My stomach churned. We could not play the numbers game. La Crescent was too big a school. But maybe victory was still ours in another way.

The statistician began to announce the boys' teams from last place to first. He read off town after town, but I didn't hear Wykoff. I was hearing Lanesboro, Lewiston, Caledonia, and Rushford, but I still didn't hear Wykoff. Then I heard Spring Valley, but *not* Wykoff.

I didn't know there were so many teams in the district. The statistician's voice droned on. *Maybe we're so small a team they're neglecting us all together.*

My whole team was tense, and we grabbed each other's shoulders.

Would Wykoff be read next? . . .

"Third place," echoed the loudspeaker.

Who would be third place? Would it be us? Us?

"The third-place finisher," the statistician repeated, "is *Preston.*"

There was a shriek in my ears. *My* team cheered with joy. They picked me up in the air. *We were the district runner-up!*

135

. . . But all that had been last year. This year was different.

The rain pelted my body as I sloshed through the mud, making the lonely walk back to the bus. I could see the boys getting into the car taking them back to the senior class trip in Minneapolis.

Had that trip hurt us as a team?

I don't think it helped us, but I can't say it hurt us either. Four seniors on that trip, Mike, Reed, Pete, and Sam, had smashed the school record in the 1600 meter relay today.

I trudged up the steps and slipped into the bus. Last year I had cradled a trophy under my arm. This year my arms were empty, even though everyone expected me to bring a trophy back to Wykoff.

It was like Christmas when I was a kid. One Christmas was so dazzling, so beautiful, so joyous that I expected the next Christmas to be the same; but it wasn't the same, and because it wasn't I had an empty feeling.

Last year, when we were runner-up, everything was so dazzling, so beautiful, so exciting. But this year wasn't the same. No runner-up trophy.

I found my spot in the front of the bus. Kenny smiled at me. I grimaced back at him. What would I do without our bus driver? He was an image of strength. And his strong smile made me think twice about my sadness.

What had gone wrong with our "best season ever"? We had done our very best at Conference, with a strong will to win, and finished fourth. We likewise ran our hearts out at District. But no trophy.

Yes, we were handicapped by our size, but I had forgotten that no matter how "good" you are, there is always someone else better.

The bus was quiet, but it was a relieved quiet.

Don, the shot putter and discus thrower, smiled at me. He was district champion today. Maybe I shouldn't be sad.

But what do you do when your "Christmas" isn't as merry as last "Christmas"?

I began to realize that no two days are ever alike. The joy we find in one day won't be found in another. But joy will be found in any day if you will look for it. We should not compare the strengths of yesterday to the weaknesses of today.

We did not win a trophy. But Sam was still undefeated. Our team still boasted district champions. And both boys and girls were going on to regional competition. We weren't runner-ups, but we had finished high—third place. That was not bad for the smallest track school in the district—the school with the clay and mud track. And this season, fourteen school records were broken.

The bus rumbled back to Wykoff. For most of the people the season was over. A few would carry on our rugged tradition at regionals.

There was no trophy on that bus. Instead, there were *many* trophies. Each young man and woman was a dazzling, beautiful, and joyous trophy.

What About You?

Do you find "dazzling trophies" even when expected trophies don't appear? This year we had to learn that lesson.

We had to look a little harder and in different places to find this year's trophy.

No two days are ever alike. The joy that is found in one day will not likely be found in another. But joy will be found in any day if you will look for it.

"This is the Lord's doing; it is marvelous in our eyes. This is the day which the Lord has made; let us rejoice and be glad in it" (Ps. 118:23–24, RSV).

1. Has a "Christmas" or some special event you thought would be great ever flopped for you?
2. Do you believe joy can be found in any day if you look for it?
3. Does God or do you "make" your days?
4. Have you ever had a perfect day? Is it realistic to expect any day to be perfect?
5. What can you do to properly appreciate each day God gives you?

33

When You Are Weak,
Then You Are Strong

Two other girls had advanced to regional competition with her. Now the events of those two girls were over. They had not placed; only Janie remained.

She leaned forward, her eyes penetrating down the long runway to the smoothed-out rectangle of sand, so far away.

She could hear the clapping hands, the laughter, the shouts, the sudden eerie pockets of silence which were all a part of the colorful Minnesota crowd now packing the stadium.

This would be her last jump. And as she chewed on that thought, another flashed into her mind.

I could be the first girl in my town and school to score in regional competition. The first!

She blasted forward, her feet stabbing the runway. Her heart aflame with vigor. Her eyes ignited by dreams . . .

. . . The emergency coaches' meeting was very crowded. And the post-meet atmosphere was mixed with both elation and depression.

"I protest the girls' long jump," one coach said, anger rising in his voice. "I measured the size of the take-off board and it's *not* regulation length. It has to be regulation size before the long jump is officially valid, and for the two first-place finishers to go on to state. I protest," he seethed out. "I demand that we do the girls' long jump over . . ."

. . . I could be the first, she thought. *The first girl in my town to place in regional competition!*

Her feet beat the runway. That rectangle of sand zoomed toward her. Closer. Closer!

But she could see past the sand into a misty vision. She could see her dream . . .

". . . But how can we run the long jump over?" asked another coach standing in the crowd. "The medals have all been handed out."

"I agree," a third coach said. "Besides, many of the girls that have placed have already gone home."

"I say that we do the long jump over on Monday," the protesting coach barked out. "In a neighboring town, with a regulation board . . ."

The first girl! The first girl from Wykoff!

The take-off board raced toward her, striking at her feet. Step! Step! Step! Pound!

Her foot launched from the board . . .

". . . That board is illegal," the coach protested. "Let's do the event over on Monday, at another town, in a legitimate long-jump pit . . ."

. . . Janie leaped; her powerful legs carried her high into the air. She rode on the crest of conquest, peaking at the height of her vision, viewing the world of reds and blues, tears, sweat, laughter, shouts . . .

. . . .Down! Down! Down! Falling to a land of dreams. Her body soared forward as her legs reached out before her. She stretched and pulled and groaned, using every muscle, every hope, every pain.

The earth zoomed at her with tremendous speed.

Reach! The first!

Crash!

Sand flew all about her. In a storm of fury Janie pulled her whole body forward.

Silence. The verdict?

"Measure!"

I've done it!

". . . Her jump is illegal," the protesting coach said.

"Nothing goes right for a Wykoff track woman!" an ugly voice screamed inside her. "*Nothing*. The whole world's against you."

The meet was over and Janie went home.

Janie placed fifth in the long jump. Her jump was not declared illegal.

She was part of a small track team with a clay and mud track. In comparison to the other cities, of bigger teams, flashy facilities, and first-place excellence, she stood weak.

But her weakness was our strength.

The other coaches decided that because it was not the long jumper's fault for competing on an illegal take-off board, the long jump would stand as legal. Janie, therefore, became our first girl to place in regional competition in any sport. Her weakness enabled her team to have its "best season ever."

What About You?

Paul said, "When I am weak, then I am strong." He did not say, "When I am weak, then I will be made strong."

No wonder he could rejoice in all things.

"For the sake of Christ, then, I am content with weaknesses, insults, hardships, persecutions, and calamities; for when I am weak, then I am strong" (2 Cor. 12:10, RSV).

1. What does the above Bible passage mean to you?
2. How can your weakness be strength?
3. If Christianity became weak in this country by being declared illegal, what would you do?
4. Can you think of a weak accomplishment in your life that is really a strong accomplishment?
5. What can you do to enable your weakness to become God's strength?

34

Running Ragged Makes Rugged

The champion had been written up in newspaper articles and lauded by television stories. And yes, many colleges were interested in him. *He* was the champion. Undefeated.

This year the champion was from Wykoff.

For two years Sam had learned, worked, believed, failed, and this year, in track meet after track meet, week after week, he had *won*. Other hungry hurdlers, as hungry as he had been last year, wanted with all their heart to beat him.

The regional track meet!

Two years ago he had been here as a spectator. But today his dream had become reality.

His eyes drank in the bright colors and the anticipation and the excitement of the packed stadium. He was Champion.

"Sam," I told him before the race. "You've done everything right to get here. We won't change anything now. Just don't jump the gun. One false start and it will all be over. You'll be disqualified . . ."

Sam smiled, and then nodded in a grim determination. Together we had watched too many champion hurdlers lose as a result of jumping the gun.

"Runners to your marks!"

All of the hurdlers lined up, poised in the blocks, ready to explode forward.

No false start, I thought. All these months of work and sweat and determined dreams. I could handle it if it was a loss by a hair at the finish line, but I couldn't handle a false start.

"Set!" Every hip raised. Each runner ready to dive at the sound of the gun.

This was it! If Sam won today, he would be our first region champion and would go on to state for a second year. There was still a faint whisp of a hope that this could be our "best season ever."

Gun!

The young men, their bodies aflame with the passion to win, crashed in violent, sprinting footsteps toward the first hurdle. The pack cleared the first hurdles, but Sam was not in the lead.

Why was Sam an undefeated champion? Why did Sam, despite inexperience, rugged facilities, injuries, and hundreds of obstacles, win in race after race?

Why?

Sam rebelled against the push-button, posh, lush modernism of our day. He rebelled against the spirit of "we have to have the very best and do it the easiest way or we will not do it at all."

No, Sam did not have the best team, the best track tradition, or the best track, but this did not stop him. He went forward and did his best, and today he had the chance of being the best in the region.

That was why he was undefeated.

Determination was wild in him. When I looked at the strain on his face I knew that nothing, absolutely nothing, could stop him now.

He passed one runner as he fired over a hurdle. Then he shot by another.

Last year, Sam thought, *last year another was the champion. But this year, I am the champion.*

He was dead even with the lead runners.

One hurdle! Another!

The two young men fought it out. And when they came off the next hurdle, Sam was in the lead.

The cheering swallowed him. I jumped for joy.

Hurdle! Hurdle!

Cheers!

Lean! Tape!

Region Champion! The first in Wykoff's history! The first!

What About You?

Technology has made your life easier. But life in Christ is a rugged life.

Don't watch your adventures on television; live your own adventures. Don't let computers do your thinking for you; have the mind of Christ.

God needs a rugged, new generation of Christians who will, with courage, follow wherever Christ leads. A generation that has the strength to love and be gentle, so that the world, strangled by evil, may know the living Christ.

"For we do not want you to be ignorant, brethren, of the affliction we experienced in Asia; for we were so utterly, unbearably crushed that we despaired of life itself . . . but that was to make us rely not on ourselves but on God who raises the dead" (2 Cor. 1:8–9, RSV).

1. What old things, like cars, clothes, or shoes, are you embarrassed about? Why do they embarrass you?
2. Why do we feel we must always have the newest and best things?
3. How many hours a week do you watch television? What alternative activities could you be doing?
4. If you had to be alone in the wilderness for a week, could you survive?
5. What can you do to prepare for the rugged life of Christian discipleship?

35

What If You Don't Win First Place?

This year things were different.

We did not leave Wykoff with all the fanfare we did last year. Yet a whole crowd of Wykoff people made the long drive to Bloomington for the state track meet. Pete and many others were in the stadium ready to watch Sam run. But I was on the other side of the stadium talking to Sam.

"This is it," I said. "This year we're not the hicks we were last year. Sam, my three seasons of coaching you is ending at this moment. You're on your own. You've done everything right. When that gun sounds, don't think about what you're doing; just do it. Do your best."

Three seasons, I thought. *Three seasons of work, dreams, joys, and disappointments. And now it's all down to this.*

I jogged to the other side of the stadium to be close to my friends. I sat down next to Pete, just as I had last year.

It was an extremely hot day. The sun lit up all the bright colors of the stadium packed with people.

We waited for the start of the race.

This has to be different from last year, I thought. *Last year he didn't even make finals. But the finals are about to start and Sam's getting into the blocks.*

"He *won't* win," a lying voice sneered within me. *"He'll go home again without any points. He's from too small a team, with limited facilities, with limited experience. He's too weak to stand up against the big boys."*

146

I looked down the track. Eight men were mounting the blocks, the eight best in the state of Minnesota. But only one man would finish in first place. What about the seven losers? How would they feel about themselves when the smoke cleared and the state meet was over?

Gunshot!

With tremendous speed the crowd of hurdlers fought their way down the track.

My eyes searched through the hurdlers. The final race. Not a dream. The last chance at our best season ever!

Hurdles crashed! Spikes tortured the track, but I could not see Sam.

Three years of shin splints and pulled muscles and bruises over tripped hurdles and noisy bus rides and dropped batons and cold, rainy track meets and false starts and dry heaves and gasping breaths and lost tape measures and muddy shot puts and bent cross bars and sweaty clothes and beat-up running shoes and heartaches and tears and now, now . .

. . . Sam was the only one left. The only survivor in the three-season battle. He alone had not been eliminated at district, region, and state. He stood for all that was good and worthwhile and honorable about Wykoff. He was tough, but gentle, courageous, but vulnerable, and strong despite weakness. Sam was unspoiled and did not ask for any favors from life. I could think of no better person to represent us at the state track meet. He *was* Wykoff.

I looked into the pack of runners as hurdles crashed to the earth.

Could I see him?

Was he in first place? Second? Last?

The last hurdle!

"Look!"

Heading for the tape! Sam was in the middle of three, the rest were closing up behind him. But he was surging ahead. Surging ahead!

Is he going to win?!

The screaming surged, peaked, and died out.

The race was over. The season was over. There were tears on my cheeks.

A three-step platform stood on the stadium infield. A dignified official looped a third-place medal around Sam's neck. Applause fired out of the crowd as his name was called off. Then the same thing happened with the second-place finisher and the champion.

This time Sam was not the champion. His undefeated string was broken.

When eight of the best hurdlers in the state compete in a race, even if they all do their 100 percent best, it's simple mathematics. There will still be only one winner and seven *losers*. How then should those losers feel about themselves?

"Face it," the foul voice spoke again to my soul. "Losing makes you a loser. Face it."

I'm getting so sick of that voice.

Sam threw his arms around me.

"Third place! I got third in the state!"

He had much to be proud of and nothing to be ashamed of. In three seasons, two years, he had worked himself up from a beginning hurdler to the third-best hurdler in his class in the state of Minnesota. Sam was the first person in the history of his town to place in state competition in any sport.

We were all very proud of him.

What About You?

What will you do if you don't win first place?

How will you keep your head high if your friend wants nothing to do with you, if your parents yell at you, if someone calls you "weak," if you fail at a task, if you get cut from the team, if you are never asked for a date, if you get a "D," or no one votes for you?

Remind yourself that you are a winner in God's eyes. You are so valuable and precious to Him that He has chosen *you* as a person He wants to *live inside*! He wants you for His heir!

If Christ lives in you, you will be raised above your problems. Your problems are not yours, but His.

"To them God chose to make known how great among the Gentiles are the riches of the glory of this mystery, which is Christ in you, the hope of glory" (Col. 1:27, RSV).

1. Your problem is not yours, but His; do you agree with that?
2. On what do you build your self-esteem?
3. Would you have felt the same way Sam did after winning third place, or would you have been disappointed?
4. What can you do to avert falling apart when you face the losses of life?
5. Have you let Christ live His life in you today?

36

The World Recognizes First Place

Third in the state of Minnesota!

The third best hurdler in the state of Minnesota. Quite an accomplishment for a young man who had only been hurdling for two calendar years.

But the world recognizes only the first-place winners. It ignores third-place winners.

So how would our world treat us when we return to Wykoff from the state track meet?

I drove the school car from the Twin Cities. Sam and Pete and I stopped to get an ice cream cone in Cannon Falls. Then we were back in the car traveling toward southeast Minnesota.

"It's all over," Pete said.

"Yeah," I said, turning down the car radio on that soft, spring Saturday evening. "You go on to college in the fall. And Sam here goes into the Air Force in a matter of weeks."

Sam's eyes stared out his open car window as sweet air stroked his face, whistling as it sent his hair flying. His vision was on green meadows, corn sprouting out of the earth, on far fields of sheep, cows, and horses. But his eyes were also on something else: the invisible and unknown future.

"Wonder what they'll think of all this fuss back home," he said softly, holding the medal in his hand that hung from his neck.

We drove into Rochester. And to our surprise there were antique cars cruising Broadway.

Soon we were out of the city, drawing nearer to Wykoff.

In this world, first place is always glorified, lauded, put on a pedestal. Second place is just a curiosity. Third place . . . forgotten.

"What's up ahead?" Pete asked, peering over the front seat.

"Looks like a road block," Sam said.

A long string of cars was parked on the shoulder of Highway 16—all behind a large red fire truck.

The next thing I knew Sam and I were whisked out of the school car. Then we were asked to climb up on top of the fire truck. The siren screamed, and we tore toward Wykoff. The string of cars followed us with horns honking. And when we entered Wykoff, people came out of their homes and waved.

A parade! For us?

Then the fire engine dropped us off at Wykoff's gym. Inside that gym was a celebration in Sam's honor.

Several speakers addressed the audience of well-wishers, expressing how proud they were that Sam was the third best hurdler in the state of Minnesota.

Sam's mother and father both spoke. They told the crowd how happy they were that Sam had been a part of the Wykoff track team.

I spoke. Even Pete spoke.

Then Sam talked to the people of Wykoff. His voice slow, deliberate, a glass of punch in one hand, a piece of cake in the other. "Thank you so much for caring. I'm going into the Air Force soon. I'll miss you all very much . . ."

Will the real winner please stand?

What About You?

In a larger town, a town accustomed to athletic accomplishments, a third-place winner would not have produced a parade and a celebration. But in Wykoff, Sam's feat was mighty.

If you are a great athlete, your accomplishments may look weak in the company of scholars.

If you are a great scholar, your accomplishment may look weak in the company of physical laborers.

Your weakness will be strength to some, weakness to others.

Follow Christ and you will be strong in the eyes of God.

152

"His master said to him, 'Well done, good and faithful servant'" (Matt. 25:21, RSV).

1. Your strengths may be weaknesses in the eyes of some people. Can you think of a case where this is true?
2. If God calls you strong, what do you think are His reasons?
3. Can you think of something you have done in your life you are downgrading, that should not be downgraded?
4. Describe a strong person you know. What does this tell you about your concept of strength?
5. What can you do to be strong in the eyes of God?

37

Positively Negative

The cigarette dangled from the corner of his mouth, the ash a quarter-of-an-inch long. The brim of his press-pinned slouch hat was pulled down over one dead eye. His body was wrapped in an overcoat even though the spring day was very warm. And somewhere during that rousing, happy, celebrative joyride that Sam and I took on the Wykoff volunteer fire engine, Riley Hunter fell off the truck into the gutter.

"Hunter," I said as I addressed the soiled sports writer (read or reread chapter two), "I learned a great deal about you this season."

"Hummph!" Hunter snorted, as he picked his hat from out of a mud puddle, wiping the mud off onto one of his pant legs.

"I learned that you sound like the devil himself. I can hear you in myself, in other people, and in the world's opinion. You are a condemning, critical, ugly voice. You are always negative."

Riley Hunter plopped the muddy hat onto his head. "Yeah," he laughed in a sickly wheeze. " 'Negative Negations of the News' is the name of my newspaper column."

"It seems, Mr. Hunter," I went on, "I can rebuke you, cast you out, and ignore you. These combat measures scare you and cause you to retreat for a while, but sooner or later you always slink back."

"So?" Hunter smirked, lighting up a cigarette. "What are you going to do about it?"

"Well, I haven't tried this too much, but I must say it's worked when I have tried it."

"What's that?" he asked suspiciously.

"Until Christ puts you where you belong, I'm going to make you work for me," I said.

His eyes were transformed from sleepless slits to large ovals. His jaw dropped, and the cigarette fell out of his mouth. He smiled, and then, almost in apology, he said, "Certainly you must mean that if you can't beat me you will join me?"

"*No.*"

"Oh, I get it. If you can't get rid of me, learn to live with me?"

"No, Riley Hunter. I believe that in *everything* God works for the good with those who love him, who are called according to his purpose (Rom. 8:28). Therefore, if I love God and live in His will by trusting my Savior Jesus Christ, to live His life in and through me, then even *you* can work for my good."

Fear was on his face. He backed away from me in tiny steps. "You're crazy," he croaked out.

"From now on, Mr. Riley Hunter, if I hear you scream in my life, screaming out your foul and negative language, I'm going to let your negatives remind me of God's positives and that He has a positive answer to every negative—"

"Shut up!"

"For instance," I spoke on, ignoring his outburst, "if I feel inadequate, that inadequacy is going to cause me to look at Christ as the adequacy in my life. If I feel strong dislike, or even hatred for a person, I'm going to look to the God who is love and let Him teach me how to love that person. If I feel fear, that fear's going to cause me to ask Christ who gives courage to operate in my life. If I can't forgive somebody, I'll ask Christ to show me again how He forgives. If I should feel weak, I'll remember that God is my strength, and with Christ living His life as me, in and through me, I can be strong. In fact, my weakness can be God's strength. If I feel like a loser, that feeling will remind me that I'm such a winner in God's eyes that He sent His only Son Jesus to die a brutal and ugly death for me. Losing does not make one a loser, Mr. Hunter."

"No! No!" Riley Hunter yelled. "I can't stand listening to you. You're crazy, I tell you! Absolutely crazy!" He staggered backward, limping to remove himself from me.

"I have just one more thing to say to you, Mr. Hunter."

"What's that?"

"Do I smell smoke?"

He sniffed. Then his eyes dropped to the cuff of his pant leg. His cigarette had fallen into the cuff, burning his pants.

"Aaaagh!" he shook his leg and hobbled down the street.

That was not the last I saw of Riley Hunter. But the next time I smelled him, I was ready for his invasion.

What About You?

God lets you feel your needs so He can properly communicate the fact to you that He has the supply for all your needs.

When you need courage, love, strength, or whatever else, look to God in Christ.

"I form light and create darkness, I make weal and create woe, I am the Lord, who do all these things. Shower, O heavens from above, and let the skies rain down righteousness; let the earth open, that salvation may sprout forth, and let it cause righteousness to spring up also; I the Lord have created it" (Isa. 45:7–8, RSV).

1. Do you think *you* can make "Riley Hunter" work for you?
2. What do you think about God being the positive for your negative?
3. Read *What About You?* again. Does this change your ideas about prayer? How?
4. Is it true that you can rebuke, cast out, and ignore "Riley Hunter", yet he always seems to return?
5. What negative in your life can you ask God to fill with His positive?
6. Is Christ the Savior and Lord of your life? Will you commit yourself to Him today? He has already committed himself to you.

38

As It Was Recorded

This book is based on the true accomplishments of the Wykoff track team. The following is from *Kat Tracks,* the Wykoff High School yearbook for the year in which the events of *Will the Real Winner Please Stand* took place.

"WHAT A SEASON!"
"This season turned out to be the best season ever for girls track in Wykoff. The team can be very proud of this since they had to overcome numerous injuries during the year. . . . The girls looked impressive with their small but skilled team. . . . Throughout the season the girls gave it their all and steadily improved. The hard work resulted in seven new school records. . . ."
"BEST SEASON EVER!!"

"The boys track season was the culmination of three years of hard work and determination. The end result—Wykoff's best track season ever! Competing all season against schools usually much larger, the track team defeated well over thirty schools. . . . After a tough conference meet, the team turned their attention toward the district. There they placed third, sending athletes on to regions. . . . When the points were totaled, Wykoff had placed in the top ten schools in the region. . . . But the most exciting event turned out to be Phil Kaun's continued undefeat in the 110 high hurdles, enabling him to go to state competition for the second year in a row.

"On Saturday, June 6, Phil Kaun returned to Wykoff a celebrity. Riding on a fire truck, leading a cheering motorcade of fans, Phil wore a state medal around his neck. He had placed third in the 110 high hurdles.

"Phil single-handedly put Wykoff's track team in the top thirty schools of the state, and on a points basis tied for 12th in the state. This made Wykoff the highest scoring team from the conference in state competition, and 6th highest in this region."